FULL DISSIDENCE

FULL
DISSIDENCE

NOTES FROM AN UNEVEN PLAYING FIELD

HOWARD BRYANT

Beacon Press · Boston

BEACON PRESS
Boston, Massachusetts
www.beacon.org

Beacon Press books
are published under the auspices of
the Unitarian Universalist Association
of Congregations.

23 22 21 20   8 7 6 5 4 3 2 1

This book is printed on acid-free paper that meets the uncoated paper
ANSI/NISO specifications for permanence as revised in 1992.

Text design by Michael Starkman at Wilsted & Taylor Publishing Services

A section of "Renters" was adapted from Howard Bryant,
"In Controversial Year, Cubs-Indians Classic a Finale MLB Needed,"
ESPN.com, November 10, 2016.

Library of Congress Cataloging-in-Publication Data
Names: Bryant, Howard, author.
Title: Full dissidence : notes from an uneven playing field / Howard
    Bryant.
Description: Boston : Beacon Press, 2020. | Includes bibliographical
    references.
Identifiers: LCCN 2019026263 (print) | LCCN 2019026264 (ebook) |
    ISBN   9780807019559 (hardcover) | ISBN 9780807019665 (ebook)
Subjects: LCSH: Political culture—United States. | Civil rights—United
    States. | Identity politics—United States. | Political
    corruption—United States. | Business and politics—United States. |
    United States—Politics and government—2017–
Classification: LCC JK1726 .B79 2020 (print) | LCC JK1726 (ebook) |
    DDC 306.20973—dc23
LC record available at https://lccn.loc.gov/2019026263
LC ebook record available at https://lccn.loc.gov/2019026264

For Tisa

CONTENTS

INTRODUCTION

To be black is to be a dissident. At some unspecific point over the past quarter century, and likely long before, America convinced me of this. The seismic wreckage of Ferguson, the daily, microscopic humiliations produced first by the pollsters who reveal that high percentages of whites believe black people have it *better* than whites *and* then later by the ones who think we deserve our wretched conditions, certainly confirmed it. Democrat or Republican, protestor or appeaser, lover or fighter, black life in America is one of navigation, for the moment black people issue a grievance of any size, the white mainstream backlash is loud and swift, the strategies and tactics we have employed to find acceptance as Americans collapse—and we are told we can go back to Africa.

The thought stuck, as important thoughts do, and as a result the traditional framings of and solutions to racial questions in this country felt increasingly insufficient, limiting, patronizing. There has been so much shrapnel. The historical arc of black triumph followed by harsh white response was not only instructive in understanding the big issues, such as Reconstruction or the half century of mobilized white response to *Brown v. Board of Education*, but it also felt very much a part of a menacing present marked by the throaty and effusive rejection of history itself. Even at this late date, despite decades of taxpayer-funded data to the contrary, countless funerals and billions of dollars in taxpayer-funded civil lawsuits, Americans still argue whether police interact with black citizens with more hostility and violence. Americans, twenty years into the fifth century of European inhabitance, still debate whether its white founders intended a nation by white people, for white people—even though the foundations of this country can be routinely found in any eighth-grade history textbook. This country is proud to accept nothing of its own past. It cannot even get the basics right, and it is exhausting.

Dissidence can never be a place of origin but is rather a destination, a conclusion after the long journey that faith—in the ballot, the corporate partnerships, the diversity and inclusion initiatives, the Rooney Rules, or just America's belief in its own exceptionalism—is no longer an option, and was probably never a particularly good one in the first place. It is the realization that our conventional strategies and solutions have been, if not illegitimate, then failures of mission. It is a break with the mainstream, and a finding of comfort living outside of it.

This book addresses that beginning following the end of exhaustion, a collection of essays that examine varied spaces of the front lines: blackness, where advocating for black people is treated as a punishable offense and, in a time of increasing hostility from the locker room to the White House, one of insurrection; of an authoritarian state, where no amount of evidence or video or debt will shake Americans from their fidelity to police at home and a runaway war machine abroad; to surrender relinquishing the concept of public wealth and to the acceptance of corruption as a value, all enveloped in a vapid but influential celebrity culture.

This collection of essays is not a how-to survival guide for a darkening time but an individual response to the malignant behaviors that have enveloped us. They are, at the end of the journey, a declaration of rejection.

ORIGINS

Once, appearing on ESPN to discuss the controversy of Colin Kaepernick not voting, I suggested that instead of his abstinence disqualifying his say on the American situation, perhaps he had gone "full dissident" and recognized the accepted framework of sociopolitical involvement—the ride-alongs with cops, the listening to candidates owned by money, the insistence that deliberate, institutional racism is just a misunderstanding still unsorted—and found them useless. I further argued that if he saw an unredeemed, corrupt system as the problem, there was no reason for him to trust in it and even less reason to expect him to participate in it.

Full dissidence may or may not have applied to Kaepernick, but it certainly felt personal. The thoughts were neither new nor revelatory, certainly not to me or any black person who reaches a certain age, a certain rage or breaking point, but they were nevertheless true: Donald Trump's installation as president was a proud and unhidden repudiation of the nation's first black president, and no matter how many attempts at misdirection toward economic anxiety or some other, greater complex phenomenon, some element of taking back proprietorship of the country had appealed to an overwhelming number of white people who voted for him. With Trump's lies and distortions normalized by an overmatched, often complicit free press, the writer Michiko Kakutani referred to his presence as "the death of truth." Dozens of books followed along similar themes regarding the decline of standards and accountability, but underneath so much of the apparent discontent, from Charleston to Charlottesville, is an anti-blackness, a reminder of to whom the country belongs. This was a reclaiming.

I do not say this hyperbolically, but Trump's election felt like a repudiation of a half century of black assimilation and aspiration to integration, of lifetimes of relationships, and of strategies and choices to better navigate the maze of white America. It didn't *feel* personal. It *was* personal. Something was dying, though at first I could scarcely pinpoint what, since I did not possess previously any great belief in this country's commitment to black equality, either on a state or personal level. In other words, I was already down following the election but I did not have far to fall.

But whatever lack of faith I may have possessed in the colorblind, Utopian future, millions of black families *did* believe in it, and they risked their children to the aspirational pathways, whether rooted in the Christian ethics of kindness and compassion or in the possibilities of education. Central to that belief was the strategy of moving their families away into hostile white communities of Milwaukee and Long Island, placing their children into hostile school systems in Boston or Denver, for the purpose of better. Acceptance. Citizenship. This was the endgame to the faith, and the twin acts of the triumph of the Obama presidency, the Trump corrective, and the proud amorality that followed killed it.

Black success, those who choose to listen know, has always led to white retribution, whether that success was something as revolutionary as Barack Obama addressing the crowd at Grant Park that night in 2008 or the unremarkable victory of an average black person scoring a decent job. What died was the belief that a day without white retribution was ever possible, replaced by the more immediate sentiment that it no longer mattered.

None of this, it should be noted, was theoretical. Some of my longtime white friends had already revealed themselves and decades-long friendships turned to dust. Skirmishes began as bee stings: the female friend I had known since seventh grade who told me in October 2008 that Sarah Palin was smarter and more qualified to be president than Obama; the thirty-year friend who before Trump's inauguration told me how "disappointed" he was in the civil rights icon John Lewis for calling out Trump's weakly coded racism. There were the progressive friends who, wounded and horrified by the election's outcome, had threatened to move to Canada, then in the next sentence dreaded the upcoming Thanksgiving dinner where they would have to listen to relatives revel in Trump's victory. It was as if all they had lost was a Super Bowl bet, but the decision to no longer sit at the table was rarely a consideration. These were no longer exchanges to be survived but telegrams urging a goodbye that needed to be listened to. Instead of anxiety, these departures were welcome, ballast being dropped.

Trump's election ended relationships and friendships, with family and romantic, and the referendum was not on him but on the dozens of millions people who voted for him, people whose lives, whether directly or indirectly would become part of mine. That the racism Trump promoted and condoned was occurring simultaneously with the ongoing demand that black people embrace postracialism as America's new reality represented an even greater insult for those sprinklings of black families living in predominately white communities.

That such reconsiderations were occurring nationwide, I had no doubt. I also had no doubt that the relationships it did not end made me more skeptical of the people involved, for both he and his election signified to me a stark and nonnegotiable collision of belief systems. For fleeting moments I even felt envious of those whites who could afford the luxury of being "apolitical"—of the world just not mattering that much—until I focused on the potential explanations: only whiteness and fealty to it could be strong enough to bond people of such disparate values, or those people really did not possess any values at all.

I, and the black people around me who were equally weary of this dance, did not have that luxury, and even if the number of friends who voted for Trump could be counted on one hand (at least the ones who volunteered their candidate honestly), they were not the only people who constituted my life, for they were connected by friendship, blood, and marriage to some of the sixty-two million other people who did vote for him. It was finally clear: what had died was negotiation.

By electing Trump they showed us who they were, just as the violent reaction in the 1970s by whites to black children desegregating Boston schools reminded my aunts and uncles exactly what white people had thought of them. "How much," my uncle would tell me, "they hated us." For the black families who lived in the white world, had bought the house and integrated the white community and its schools, had bought into the dream, the questions now stood even taller and more imposing. How many more Thanksgiving dinners could one be expected to sit through with one's white friends under the realization that not nearly enough questions had ever been asked of them? How, then, could one assess the people who have stayed by your side, the ones expected to attend your funeral? The ones with whom you have shared your holidays and your home and your bed and who, at any moment, could and would retreat—because, for white people, race is and always will be just a topic to either be addressed or ignored. Was it possible to trust the complicated relationships with white women, whose attitudes regarding interracial relationships seemed to be rooted in the attitude "If you're OK with me, everything's OK," yet who could always return to the comfort of whiteness when life with you got too tough?

What was being said in these relationships, in effect, was that white people wanted the benefit of loving someone black without confronting the conditions that make life difficult for black people. When white people would say to me, "I don't care if you're black," they were not being generous. They were not being progressive. They literally meant what they said. They did not care, and even if they did not mean it cruelly, they meant to say the historical, overwhelming conspiracy on the part of their country—by government, the judiciary, the financial and educational institutions, and by law enforcement—to ensure a black underclass was not enough (or was too much) for them. They might be sympathetic. They might not, but it was life, and however terrible they may have felt individually, they would do nothing more about it.

Doing nothing more about it did not only mean a willful misunderstanding of the black journey but an abandonment of the white people who *were* willing to risk their lives because they knew exactly the depth of the conspiracy and its inevitable destructiveness. The Andrew Goodmans and Michael Schwerners, William Lewis Moores and James Reebs, Viola Liuzzos, Bruce Klunders, and Heather Heyers on a national level and the few committed, important people of our anonymous lives were equally betrayed by this daily cynicism as much as any black person.

These friends and lovers, especially the lovers, sought to absolve themselves of guilt for their systemic advantages by loving the black person in their life—without risking anything to keep that person safe. They wanted to save themselves by appearing to save me, and as any black man who has dated a white woman knows, white women believe they can have both—all the preferential treatments and patriarchy of whiteness while believing in their inherent innocence. They could expose their black friends or lovers to their family's casual racism at Thanksgiving with no intention of risking their comfort, for the minority is always expected to willingly absorb humiliation as part of the privilege of the invite—but by doing this, the very people who pledged love for you with their words were sending another message by their lack of deed: they were always willing to sacrifice you.

1. FULL DISSIDENCE

WHAT COLIN KAEPERNICK TAUGHT US

Hating labor and labor unions is America's unofficial pastime. When a star athlete signs a multimillion-dollar contract, the talk radio lines explode with fans deconstructing the value of the deal, protecting the billionaire team owner's money as if it were their own. Striking teachers immediately face the cries that they shouldn't complain about their wages because they get the summers off. When football players, after years of providing entertainment for couch potatoes nationwide, sue their leagues for not disclosing the devastating health risks accompanied with the fame of stardom, those same fans, who bought the jerseys and asked for the autographs, turn coldly against their former heroes and say things like "Nobody put a gun to their head." Americans expect workers to take what they get. If you don't like it, leave. Or as they say in the NFL, next man up.

As it has for the past forty years, the Supreme Court has been the agent most enthusiastically willing to codify antiworker water-cooler sentiment into law. In May 2018 it voted 5–4 in *Epic Systems v. Lewis* to prohibit workers from joining in class-action lawsuits against their employers. A month later, in another 5–4 ruling, the court broke nearly a half century of precedent with *Janus v. American Federation of State, County and Municipal Employees, Council 31*, in which it stated that public-sector union members were not required to pay mandatory fees even though those individuals were covered by and benefited from collective-bargaining units.

The effect of these two rulings was catastrophic for unions. The first forces employees to file individual grievances against the multibillion-dollar behemoths that are their employers— even if one infraction applies to large numbers of employees. The effect of the ruling diminishes the strength-in-numbers strategies employees need in order to challenge a corporation. Intimidated and further exposed to retaliation, workers would be less likely to go it alone in a lawsuit against their bosses. The high court endorsed making it easier to silence workers.

In the second ruling, *Janus* hits labor in the wallet in an attempt to put unions out of business. By allowing some employees not to pay union dues for the workplace protections they achieved through collective bargaining while others do, the court effectively reduced the dollar amounts unions could raise to fight on behalf of their members and drove a wedge into the workforce. Who would pay union dues if they could receive the same protections for free? "There is no sugarcoating today's opinion," wrote dissenting justice Elena Kagan. "The majority overthrows a decision entrenched in this Nation's law—and in its economic life—for over 40 years. As a result, it prevents the American people, acting through their state and local officials, from making important choices about workplace governance. And it does so by weaponizing the First Amendment, in a way that unleashes judges, now and in the future, to intervene in economic and regulatory policy." A report by the Economic Policy Institute stated that *Janus* was the most impactful case on labor in the past seventy years. So much for precedent. So much for a fair fight.

Janus suffocated a union's ability to raise money and divided the workforce. *Epic Systems* limited the ability of employers to sue companies, furthering a 2011 decision preventing consumers and employees from combining forces for class-action suits against corporations. "Forced to face their employers without company," Justice Ruth Bader Ginsburg wrote in her *Epic* dissent, "employees ordinarily are no match for the enterprise that hires them." It is a coordinated attack.

Labor has no friends—not in the courts and not in the stands at sporting events, where fans routinely condemn players for earning enormous sums of money for a short period of time yet condone billionaire owners' greed. Labor barely has allies among itself, evidenced by the frequency with which union members lash out more harshly at their own ranks and ideals than at the controlling forces that destroy their foundations. During the 2010 midterm elections Barack Obama engaged in this get-tough farce by advocating the firing of teachers as a response to underperforming schools. This at a time when the profession often barely pays a living wage. Teachers' unions responded by demanding that Obama fire his education secretary, Arne Duncan. Donald Trump's 2018 tax bill lined the wallets of the rich while preventing teachers who spent their own money on school supplies from getting it back.

When Colin Kaepernick first took a knee in August 2016, both in protest of the people being killed by police and the extraordinary disinterest the legal system had in prosecuting them, I understood the attacks, from the hardhats whose first instincts were to call black people unpatriotic, to the white ex-player punditry who knew to pander to the white fan base that thinks it owns the players, to the black mainstream who feared full dissidence because it would leave them homeless and who needed to believe that the courts, the cops, and reasonable white people would be allies once they saw the dashcam footage of Tamir Rice being blown away at point-blank range.

The criticisms I found more frustrating came from people who believed Kaepernick's situation could have been avoided if only he were backed by a stronger union. Ostensible sympathizers treated the NFL Players Association as a punch line. During his struggle, they asked the question, "Where was the union?" The NFLPA was not without issues, but criticizing it served as a way for people to condescend toward the players as if their own lives were not in the anti-labor crosshairs. With workplace and First Amendment freedoms across the United States suffering an onslaught so complete the *Nation* accused the Supreme Court of creating a "Bosses' Constitution," fans should have asked, "Where was I?" Kaepernick provided a metaphor for America along so many fault lines that talking about him really meant talking about us.

"*Where was I?*"

COLIN KAEPERNICK TAUGHT US WHO IS BOSS.

The courts, state and federal governments, and the public conspired to create a deadly, union-busting apparatus, but workers are being leveled by another secret weapon: the employees themselves. They routinely speak the language of management, protect it, and while taking their daily bludgeoning at work concluded that Kaepernick deserved a bludgeoning, too.

They've been well conditioned: teachers trashed teachers unions despite nonstop local and national cuts to education. *Janus* allowed employees to trash unions *and* benefit from them. When workers finally had enough, even progressives trashed protest (*Wasn't there another way to do it?*). Weekend warriors, seized by the carbon monoxide of anti-unionism pumped into their cubicles, weaponized their own impotence, refining it into anger toward Kaepernick (*If I ever did that at MY job . . .*). In 2019, Delta Air Lines got into the spirit of *Janus* by launching a hideous union-busting ad campaign, urging its employees to spend money on football, baseball, and video games instead of paying union dues.

Even the millionaire ballplayers, the envy of unions everywhere, routinely turned on one another. During the mid-2000s, when NFL owners began rewarding rookie players with record contracts, veteran players did not band together against the front offices but directed their rage at their younger, untested teammates, as if those players had signed themselves to ridiculously unfair deals. The veterans resented the rookies publicly and privately for outearning them, and during the 2011 collective-bargaining talks they demanded ownership impose a cap on their teammates' wages, negotiating a "rookie wage scale." Rookies of similar draft slots were then hit with uniform multiyear contracts that could not be renegotiated until a player's *fourth* year. (The average NFL career, incidentally, lasts three years.)

By attacking themselves instead of the billionaires writing the checks and the front offices that decided who received them, the NFL players were only following another group of workers: NBA players. Nearly twenty years earlier the Milwaukee Bucks signed 1994 overall top pick Glen Robinson to a ten-year, $67.5 million contract before he'd ever scored his first basket. Like in the NFL, players correctly viewed the rise of rookie money as an obvious attempt to squeeze veterans' salaries, but, like in the NFL, the players went after their own. The next year, bitter veteran NBA players pushed for a rookie wage scale, essentially volunteering to cap the earning power of other players. The next season, under the new scale, top pick Joe Smith signed a mandatory three-year, $8.5 million deal. An analysis by Derek Rowe, then at the Duke University School of Law, found over the next two decades that rookie players, especially young superstars such as Kawhi Leonard, were "significantly underpaid" considering their immediate impact on their teams.

Americans patted themselves on the back for being loyal patriots to the flag with one hand while slicing their own wrists at work with the other. Fans bought the camouflage jerseys and chanted "USA! USA!" in the stands, but they were not being loyal to their country nearly as much as they were serving American corporations. Kaepernick's banishment from the NFL was a resounding victory for antiworker capitalism, another death blow to labor by its own hand. Workers across the country, many in the very locker rooms Kaepernick once occupied, abandoned him under the pretense that management was omnipotent, that *the bosses can do whatever they want*. It was the corporation that decided what was acceptable. J. J. Watt, the great Houston Texans defensive end, could raise $40 million for Hurricane Harvey relief, Major League Baseball would play a benefit game in Puerto Rico to raise money for recovery from Hurricane Maria or wear patches after the Parkland massacre, and Pittsburgh Steelers head coach Mike Tomlin could survey the wreckage and poverty in Haiti—but only as *humanitarians*. Should any player point the finger—at parties or individual policies that contribute to economic and natural disasters or gun violence—their leagues, its media business partners, and the public would punish them for being *political*. Players could provide the bandage but were forbidden from preventing the wound. Fans spoke the language of the corporation better than the CEOs spoke for themselves. Much of the public response to Kaepernick aligned with the Supreme Court's acquiescence to corporations, whether the issue was runaway political money in the infamous, corporations-are-people-too *Citizens United* case or the twin assaults of *Epic Systems* and *Janus*: we serve the rich. The corporation owes you nothing. You *are* nothing. It is an attitude embodied by the NFL's most successful team, the New England Patriots, whose soulless team motto is the gray and joyless *Do Your Job*. By burying Kaepernick for exercising his First Amendment rights, the corporation of the NFL punished democracy without showing any responsibility to it or respect for it. It was the worker, the poor slob who erroneously saw himself as next in the line of kings who did the work, who knelt to the cops during yet another Law Enforcement Appreciation Night, yet demanded nothing of the bosses who undermined the entire operation.

Consumers and a dutiful media allowed the NFL to commodify the American flag in its stadiums, to profit from it both in real and social currency while disregarding its meaning. Whether frozen with fear, fatally enamored of money, or just too selfish to have their Sunday fun and games interrupted, the public refused to link the falling democracy with the rise of the corporation. I do not believe the public lacked the ability to think critically, but rather that confronting the implications was simply too great. Better to just survive.

COLIN KAEPERNICK TAUGHT US
BLACK ATHLETES ARE SCARED TO DEATH.

West Virginia has voted Republican in every presidential election since 2000, by successively larger margins each time. Donald Trump won West Virginia in 2016 by a college football score, 69 percent to 27 percent over Hillary Clinton. Trump won Oklahoma's seven electoral votes by a similar blowout, 65 percent to 29 percent. Neither state could ever be mistaken for a stronghold of blue-wave activism. Oklahoma became a state in 1907. In its entire history, Democrats have carried it only twice, in 1948 and 1964.

Yet in 2018 teachers in both states staged mass walkouts over declining working conditions. West Virginia, which ranked between forty-sixth and fiftieth in several key academic categories, saw its teachers strike in February. Oklahoma ranked forty-third in the nation in per-student spending. Classroom sizes swelled as teacher shortages mounted. Teacher salaries were not competitive regionally or nationally. Between 2008 and 2015, the Oklahoma Policy Institute reported, the state slashed per-student spending by 23.6 percent, the largest reduction in the nation.

In Oklahoma, there's an excellent chance that the teachers in any given classroom aren't even qualified to be there. During the 2011–12 school year, the state issued thirty-two emergency teaching certificates, filling shortages with instructors who either did not have degrees in education or had not completed the state's certification process. During the 2017–18 school year, the number ballooned to 1,975. On April 2, 2018, Oklahoma's teachers followed West Virginia's and went on strike. Three weeks later, in Arizona, another red state that, except for Bill Clinton in 1996, had voted Republican in every presidential election since 1952, twenty thousand teachers walked out for a week, returning to school a week later with a 20 percent pay increase. They had won.

West Virginia comprises fifty-five counties. For nearly two weeks, the teachers refused to work in any of them, shutting down every public school in the state. They went to Charleston, inside the state capitol. On March 7 the West Virginia legislature voted a 5 percent pay increase for the teachers. They, too, had won.

In Oklahoma, after protesting at the statehouse for nine days, the teachers also could declare victory, winning $6,000 raises and additional pay increases for administrative workers. The Oklahoma teachers won even though the state is notoriously anti-union. Like in *Janus*, mandatory union membership in Oklahoma is illegal, but nonpaying union members were entitled to Oklahoma's hard-fought pay raises.

Donald Trump also won Florida, albeit, unlike in the West Virginia and Oklahoma landslides, by a 1 percent margin. Florida is a hostile place where the notorious "stand your ground" gun laws, in which people are allowed to use force to protect themselves from perceived threats, have led to the killings of innocent, unarmed people and made national headlines. Unlike Nevada's interpretation of stand your ground, Florida allows citizens to kill even if a potential assailant no longer poses a threat. Florida embraces being defined by gun culture.

On Valentine's Day 2018, Nikolas Cruz, a student at Marjory Stoneman High School in Parkland, Florida, opened fire on school grounds, killing seventeen students and faculty. CNN reported twenty-three school shootings in the first twenty-one weeks of 2018, and while the country grew numb to school shootings *("Thoughts and prayers . . .")*, students took to the streets, creating the March for Our Lives, which became a nationwide movement of school walkouts and political action. A paralyzed country suddenly was aware of the kids in the streets. Following the Sandy Hook massacre, in which twenty-six people were murdered, twenty of them first-graders, Shannon Watts, once a stay-at-home mother, organized the gun-law-reform group Moms Demand Action and did what corrupted, compromised elected officials could not and would not do: battled face to face with the National Rifle Association. In a country criminally weak on guns, twenty-nine states passed stronger gun laws. Even the NRA, brazen and boorish and seemingly invincible, hounded by the seemingly overmatched Parkland kids and the moms who'd had enough, shut down its propaganda wing, NRA TV.

It was a start and a reminder that the outraged Facebook posts, the smarmy Twitter rants and cop-controlled ride-alongs were no match for people actually getting off of their first-world asses and taking to the streets. Americans have often forgotten it, but policies change when the bodies start blocking traffic—or entry into the state house. In two of the states most hostile to unions, the teachers won. In another state that protects guns more than it protects citizens, the students won. Against the all-powerful gun lobby, the moms won. They won by showing their faces for two weeks in the halls of power—on the steps of the legislature, in the statehouse rotunda, in the faces of the powerful—across the country, making themselves seen and heard. They were not just griping on Facebook, writing their local congressperson or retweeting on Twitter, but were in the street. They were seen, physically. They could not be ignored. Even New England Patriots owner Robert Kraft, who contributed a million dollars to Donald Trump's inauguration—money that maintains the NRA stranglehold on policy and held the line on Kaepernick's expulsion—loaned his private plane to the Parkland students.

When tallying the activism, the scoreboard said one thing while the public narrative said something decidedly different. The scoreboard showed an active public of teachers, students, professional organizers, mothers, poets, and writers challenging institutions from the police to state education. The people were moving. Yet scanning the culture, one might believe it was the athletes, from Colin Kaepernick to Malcolm Jenkins to LeBron James, who were bringing America along with it. Media even had a name for their resurgence: *Athlete activism*, they called it, and they were linked to courageous deeds of the past, to names like Muhammad Ali, Tommie Smith, John Carlos, and Jackie Robinson.

The players, however, were not on the frontlines at all. They had money. They had the cameras following them. They got the headlines but in actuality they were not only far more timid than the anonymous, striking math teacher from Tulsa; in many ways they went out of their way to undermine the real power of the movement.

When Kaepernick knelt, he was lauded for his courage while simultaneously being criticized for not leaning in. Protest, several players said, was ineffective compared to the power of the celebrity-athlete class, which needed only to make a phone call to secure a meeting with a high-ranking politician. Their sentiment could be reduced to a single sentence: *You can't just take a knee.* Charles Barkley said it. While working with legislators on prison reform, Malcolm Jenkins said it. While serving on panel discussions at Harvard, NFL players Devin and Jason McCourty said it, and now, in partnership with the NFL, Jay-Z said it. While doing absolutely nothing, Dallas Cowboys quarterback Dak Prescott said it, serving up a paragraph of Michelin Star–level word salad to the *Dallas Morning News* on July 27, 2018:

> I respect what all those guys believe in. If they believe it's going to make a change and it's going to make a difference then power to them. But for me, I believe in doing something, action. It's not about taking a knee. It's not necessarily about standing. We can find a different place to make our country better. And obviously I'm not naive and I'm very aware of the injustice that we have going on, but I'm about the actions that we can do to fix it rather than the silent protest.

Prescott said, however, he wasn't working on any kind of action that would help raise awareness for social injustice and police brutality but was "open" to helping out in any way.

It was a clever ruse, suggesting he was beyond mere theatrics and committed to the "real work," the substantial work, but outside of himself, he wasn't fooling anyone. The players were not signaling higher commitment but rather their fear of confrontation with the owners, of the NFL and the country, which, of course, is to say the white public. They did not want to be seen in the streets, connected in the trenches of a struggle. They did not want to be named as dissidents, which is precisely what protest brings about. The millionaire, so-called athlete-activists who now had America's attention would reveal their fear through variations of the same theme: you cannot just take a knee. You have to *act*.

While the kids marched and the teachers struck—in addition to Arizona, West Virginia, and Oklahoma, teachers walked out in Los Angeles and Oakland—the players undermined them by suggesting protest was some ineffective, Selma-era relic beneath their moneyed, concierge-level access. Marching wasn't action, they said. Taking a knee wasn't action. Blocking traffic wasn't action. It was ahistorical nonsense and the players didn't even have to crack open a book to see it. All they had to do was look around at everyday people in their own country demonstrating bodies-in-the-street, showing-your-face protest that forced state governments to negotiate with schoolteachers, and it was hundreds of thousands of Puerto Ricans shoulder to shoulder and not tweet to tweet that forced its corrupt governor, Ricardo Rossello, to resign in July 2019. It was Kaepernick's physical protest that brought the NFL's billionaire owners to the bargaining table, not with him, but with the Players Coalition, the same people who said taking a knee by itself had no value.

It wasn't just the players but a uniquely American attitude that protest was for yesterday, for the hippies and the third world—or for the yellow-vested French. America had transcended protest. We were rich. We had made it.

The Players Coalition, a group of socially conscious NFL players, partnered with lawmakers and raised important issues necessary to reform the criminal justice system, such as ending cash bail, but they cannot escape that they felt the need to diminish walking a picket line or publicly demonstrating dissatisfaction. When he grew tired of criticism Jenkins would suggest there was no difference between raising a fist and taking a knee. For proof he would refer to the responses he received from angry fans. Jenkins would have been correct—if he were comparing the act of taking a knee in 2016 to raising a fist in 1968. Otherwise, there was one gesture that mobilized the industry of professional football, inflamed the president of the United States, and became a referendum on principled risk—and it was kneeling. It wasn't raising a fist that cost Kaepernick his profession, leaving him viewed by the white public as traitorous. Because taking a knee was viewed as the inflammatory gesture, raising a fist in 2018 was actually the safer move; it signaled to the public that a player was socially conscious but *not* a dissident. For all of its historical power during the civil rights movement, raising a fist in the Kaepernick generation was not dangerous at all. It suggested compromise.

The players' timidity exposed the celebrity class and its inability to come to the rescue. At the same time Prescott was doing nothing and saying less, the Meridian (Mississippi) Police Department—in the same state Prescott attended college—was in the process of firing Daniel Starks, a white police officer who had tasered and assaulted a handcuffed black suspect. Prescott willfully parroted the comments of NFL owners. He exposed himself as an employee both on third and long and also after his daily time card had been punched.

None of that is a crime, but instead of demurring, players like Prescott went on the offensive in service of their "owners," not only refusing the most powerful weapon in the activist arsenal but openly mocking it, as if protest—the weapon of Jackie Robinson and Paul Robeson, Martin Luther King Jr., Diane Nash, and John Lewis—was beneath them and their gilded, moneyed elegance. They did so to make management and the white fan base comfortable—and to take pressure off of themselves. It would have been perfectly feasible for Malcolm Jenkins and company to recognize the tactic of physical protest as an aid in the movement while they preferred to be debriefed at the statehouse. That would have been an appropriate, two-pronged attack on injustice, for despite aligning with NFL ownership, Jenkins and his coalition have admirably used their influence to work within the justice system. But by condescending to physical protest in service of their owners, these black athletes used the historically false premise that protest did not constitute "action" in order to appear reasonable. They were not reasonable. They were afraid, and the insult of it all was staggering.

COLIN KAEPERNICK TAUGHT US HOW THE NFL SEES BLACKNESS.

During the first week of August 2018 the video game giant EA Sports admitted it had erased Kaepernick's name from the lyrics of a song included in the soundtrack of its smash-hit *Madden* football franchise. After the public fury—on social media, the platforms where the young people who religiously purchase video games traffic, and in the news cycle where the older suits gauge reaction—EA admitted its wrongdoing, claimed it had made a mistake, apologized to both Kaepernick and the artist, YG, and restored Kaepernick's name to the song. They were certainly sorry—sorry anyone noticed.

During my first years at ESPN, the enormous conflicts of interest between the company's traditional journalism wing and its business of broadcasting sports was an open secret that employees believed they could rationalize away. A refrain was repeated to me often by veteran writers and editors, the gist of which was, "I've worked here for years and no one has *ever* told me what I could or couldn't write." Superficially there was no reason to believe this wasn't true, yet it was nevertheless preposterous because the culture changes the individual long before the individuals change the culture, and inside the building the editors and reporters—especially the editors—already *knew* what types of stories and what types of tones would be acceptable to management long before having to ask. They knew which ones would produce angry phone calls from Roger Goodell, Bud Selig, or David Stern, the commissioners at the time of, respectively, the NFL, Major League Baseball, and the NBA—even when they chose to do the story anyway. Corporations rely on employees self-censoring to ensure that trouble for its business relationships is kept to a minimum. Pretty much everyone working at any corporation knows where they stand upon entering the building.

The culture is no different, I suspect, at a video game powerhouse like EA Sports, where, even if the scrubbing of Kaepernick's name was not directly ordered from the highest levels of the company, the rank and file understood the implications of his name within the NFL. It is entirely plausible that either through personal offense or being a good soldier, an individual or group of individuals took it upon themselves to remove Kaepernick's name from the game, keeping EA in virtual lockstep with Kaepernick's real-world banishment. I think they all knew exactly what they were doing.

The erasure of one player paralleled the elevation of another, and while EA was getting its story straight, Ray Lewis, for years the fearsome middle linebacker of the Baltimore Ravens, was elected to the Pro Football Hall of Fame. During Kaepernick's protest, Lewis proved to be of great service to the NFL in general and the Ravens in particular by trashing him. Lewis told Kaepernick to "keep his mouth shut," allowing himself to be used as a prominent ex-player with a broadcast platform (Lewis worked at the time for ESPN) and as a black man, as protest of police brutality, at least among athletes, is considered a black issue. Whenever struggling with the specter of Kaepernick, the

NFL's overwhelmingly white ownership and its commissioner could point to Ray Lewis, who let them employ the oldest trick in the book: find a black guy to criticize another black guy.

In the eyes of the NFL and much of its fan base, Lewis was the antithesis of Kaepernick, and to them, this undoubtedly was a compliment. Football fans easily recall the Lewis show: the pregame dance, the inspirational motivational speeches, and the even-more-ferocious hits. He was part of a fearsome lineage of the prototypical NFL linebacker-as-leader, heir to the legends from Nitschke to Huff, Butkus to Singletary. His Hall of Fame induction speech was craven. I have no doubt that Lewis embodied the NFL's self-portrait. He reminds me of the person at whose jokes people laugh because they fear him. I bet there isn't a moment, even when fans laugh and nod their heads approvingly during his enshrinement, that he cannot escape his own infamous appositive—even among those in the audience who would say he's part of the NFL family. In public, to them he is Ray Lewis, Legendary NFL Hall of Famer. In private, closer to the halls of respectability, he is Ray Lewis Who Was Directly Involved in an Unsolved Double Murder. He is Ray Lewis Who Was Charged with Two Counts of Murder before pleading guilty to obstruction of justice. The moral bankruptcy of the NFL was magnified when Lewis was allowed to sermonize in his induction speech for thirty-four minutes without acknowledging what he knows took place that day in 2000. The NFL did not encourage humility or demand contrition from Lewis but actively enabled precisely the opposite: a callow and fraudulent spectacle. Lewis used the years following his involvement in the murders of Richard Lollar and Jacinth Baker in a brawl outside an Atlanta nightclub to become even louder and more self-absorbed, to become even more convinced that he has no blood on his hands simply by repeating it over and over again.

The NFL profits from this ridiculousness. Ray Lewis tells them what they want to hear because his rags-to-riches success bullshit leaves their controlling system in place, creates less resistance to its money machine of broken brains, bones, and bodies and creates fewer dissidents because of the number of friends and family who rely on muscular shoulders of the black stars who made it. By punishing the Kaepernick brain, it enabled the Lewis body, whose self-important preening is completely nonthreatening to the white owners who pay him. Nor is he a challenge to the white coaches who tell him what to do. The NFL hierarchy is comfortable profiting from the dead-or-in-jail narrative of black boys believing they have no options beyond tackling or dunking or singing that is devouring black youth. The dichotomy of Lewis being celebrated for being the ultimate football warrior while being publicly illegitimate provided the perfect mirror for the thoughtful, searching Kaepernick, whose banishment reflected the antiblackness embedded within sports, where the most successful black professionals work. Forget the victims. The more Lewises, the better.

It should come as no surprise that Kaepernick has missed at least two full seasons and counting for making a gesture while Ray Lewis, who was directly involved in an unsolved double murder, was fined $250,000 by the NFL and *never missed a game*.

COLIN KAEPERNICK TAUGHT US WE ARE DESPERATE.

September 3, 2018: Nike unveils an ad featuring an extreme closeup of Colin Kaepernick, in a black-and-white photograph, staring uncompromisingly ahead, the words "Believe in something. Even if it means sacrificing everything" superimposed across his serious and unsmiling face. Social media ignites. The pontificators pontificate about Nike, a business partner with the NFL, outfitter of the entire league, unveiling a Kaepernick ad a week before the start of the season. Within hours the details begin to trickle out of Nike's Beaverton, Oregon, headquarters: the sneaker giant has signed Kaepernick to a new endorsement deal to be a brand ambassador of sorts. The next day Nike unveils a one-minute ad voiced over by Kaepernick, news in and of itself since he has not given an interview since January 2017. It is a spell of inspiring clips of athletes, from greats to unknowns, all connected by their drive to be their very best selves and by Kaepernick, now the martyred conscience of a generation. The ad was viewed as a marketing masterstroke, cultivating the fertile, ignored constituency of Kaepernick supporters who for two years had been treated as invisible under the asphyxiating humidity of flag-waving "real fans." Something else occurs: by standing up to the NFL and rehabilitating Kaepernick, Nike had implausibly become an ally in a *resistance*.

The very thought of Nike being positioned as heroic spiraled my mood. This reaction to a corporation recognizing a profit opportunity felt inauthentic. It felt desperate. Nike had never publicly denounced the NFL for the immorality (and, by settling his collusion lawsuit for a reported sum of more than $60 million, unethical if not illegal) of blackballing Kaepernick in the first place. The company did revive Kaepernick from exile but did not do it out of solidarity with and support for one of its longtime clients. Nike never used its enormous marketing muscle power to sanction or even admonish the NFL or to send an actual financial message that it would not allow freedoms, or people, to be trampled. For two full seasons, the company said nothing. When the public vilified Kaepernick, his employers, media, and even progressive members of the Supreme Court (Ruth Bader Ginsburg, the revered "Notorious RBG," once called his protest "dumb and disrespectful") all said nothing in support. They said nothing when Donald Trump trashed Kaepernick, and it should also be noted that the company still offers discount coupons to police officers who shop online.

The ad itself was *safe*, and through its safeness, Kaepernick was no longer dangerous, or at least no longer *as* dangerous. There was no mention of his protest in the ad, nor of police, nor of any of the reasons why he was the voice of the ad. Nothing about Kaepernick's presence spoke to *justice*, for Philando Castile or Daniel Shaver, Sandra Bland or Tamir Rice, Eric Garner, or *himself*. The soccer star Megan Rapinoe, who took a knee during the national anthem in support of Kaepernick and against injustice, was shown in the ad—standing in support of the flag. For a frame, Kaepernick even spoke to the camera, standing in front of a building whose façade was covered by a hologram of the American flag. Whether through a corporate-friendly Supreme Court or profiting from the cultural collision of patriotism and protest, it was clear the American corporation was controlling the marionette. And the marionette is us.

There was something flimsy and grasping about it all, this desire to see corporations as redeeming, transformative, leading. It felt like surrender. One megacorporation (the NFL) used its ubiquity to actively punish activism and dismiss black people and their claim to full citizenship, while another (Nike) created images to inspire activism while refusing to actually support and fight for justice. Neither protest nor patriotism, it must be noted, should ever be for sale. Yet both the NFL and Nike were united in profit, the NFL cultivating the Real Americans who hated Kaepernick and Nike making his supporters, in need of hope, believe they had a corporate ally. Corporate activism is every bit the oxymoron that corporate courage is, and at its core, the selling of Kaepernick as an inspirational figure without the accompanying action of denouncing the NFL and the reckless conduct of police or of taking a tangible business risk is to profit off dead black people. At the hands of the state. To look cool. To sell sneakers. To be on the right side of history but only at the slightest of first glances.

Months later, in February 2019, when Kaepernick and the NFL settled his collusion case for a reported tens of millions, some prominent people stunningly asked if accepting the NFL's money made him a "sellout." Kaepernick did not sue the NFL for the right to protest but for the right to work. Whatever the NFL paid him was money he was owed because the league denied him the opportunity to work. Though it was not uncommon to hear that he should have given his settlement to charity, whatever monies he received from his settlement belonged appropriately to him. Kaepernick then launched a few tweets with the hashtag #TrueTo7, which through one lens could have been perceived to be a thank-you to the people who supported him during his exile and litigation but through another resembled celebrity branding. Kaepernick's power lay not in a focus on him but in his willingness to risk his career for a message where he personally was unaffected. Yet the first two years of his banishment have consisted of a social media presence that almost exclusively sells Kaepernick Nike jerseys, with him tagging and retweeting photos of people—beautiful people and plain folk alike—repping his gear or saying nice things about him. He remained equally present, committed to his Know Your Rights camps but curiously noncommittal as a public figure. What was missing was an emphasis on the continuing problem of dead black bodies at the hands of the state. The #TrueTo7 hashtag implied that justice for him was now the center of the story and not police officers being indemnified from their own police reports. In a little over a year Kaepernick had become an even more established part of the celebrity class, selling jerseys and hair-care products, with an agreement for a television show about his life with the director Ava DuVernay and, as of March 2019, a stunning streak of not having given a public interview in more than two years. Colin Kaepernick had done enough, and yet I could not help feeling conflicted for the people who had taken to the streets inspired by him, and wanting him to join them. As one New York grassroots activist said to me, "I keep hearing the term 'I'm with Kap,' but is he with us?"

COLIN KAEPERNICK TAUGHT US
HOW EXPOSED WHITE AMERICA TRULY IS.

If applauding Nike felt like surrender, was there something significant to be found in surrender? Kaepernick's physical exile from the NFL symbolized defeat, not just for his professional livelihood but for dissidence, as it was clear that the league was making an example of him. His downfall seemed a victory for corporations crushing individuals everywhere, of whiteness telling blackness to get over it, of ignoring anyone horrified that in less than a year's time, Oklahoma police officer Betty Shelby killed Terence Crutcher in the middle of the street, was acquitted of manslaughter, and then was rehired in law enforcement. Metaphorically, Kaepernick was Metacomet at Plymouth, his head on a stake as a warning for any natives with big ideas. Hearing Kaepernick anew, the voice resurrected, was there value in him, even propped up by Nike's billions, simply staying in the public's face?

Initially, I did not believe any of this to be true. I did not feel much like celebrating the maintaining of the celebrity class, especially when the Nike ads were clearly made with Kaepernick's approval and did not include protest, and did not withstand the scrutiny of a simple question: *What does any of this have to do with justice?*

Soon, stories appeared nationwide of people cutting up their Nike socks and burning their Nike sneakers, of refusing to carry Nike gear. In a spectacular fail, one Colorado storeowner went out of business. The Mississippi public safety commissioner ordered state police to no longer purchase Nike gear. A Louisiana police department dressed its suspects in Nike gear for their mug shots. The mayor of a New Orleans suburb ordered, and a Rhode Island town voted to prohibit its departments from purchasing Nike products. During the Brett Kavanaugh Supreme Court confirmation hearings, which occurred the same week Nike unveiled Kaepernick, Trump gave a speech suggesting all protesting be illegal.[1]

As news reports of schools threatening to boycott Nike and municipalities refusing to the purchase the company's apparel increased, my mind began to shift. It was clear that a man who had broken no laws and had only spoken his mind was being actively destroyed by the public. And let's be clear: by public, I mean to say the overwhelmingly white public, and the government. How else does one assess local politicians and law enforcement officers suddenly sufficiently emboldened to undertake an intimidation campaign against one of the world's most powerful corporations? Though he essentially lives on the fringes of the

American mainstream, not speaking publicly, not playing in the NFL, and not organizing protest, so many whites were exposing themselves by their disproportional response to the specter of Kaepernick.

Despite Nike's corporate duplicity, the fight could not be decoupled from Kaepernick. There was no way out. Parsing percentages of the opposition's size is a game at which Americans are expert, especially when those in power are indicted. (See: "not *all* cops," "not *all* men," and "not *all* white people.") It is an exercise in tedium but some large portion of this America had decided that Colin Kaepernick had no right to any semblance of a life, a career, or a public presence in any form. They had resolved to destroy him personally, as well as any entity associated with him, even a corporation as enormous and ubiquitous as Nike. In the summer of 2019, when Nike pulled a limited-edition Independence Day shoe because Kaepernick reportedly objected to its featuring the Betsy Ross flag, designed at a time when all thirteen colonies were slaveholding, Arizona governor Doug Ducey announced he would eliminate the financial incentives Nike was to receive for building a new plant in the Phoenix suburbs, risking local jobs and economic growth for the city of Goodyear. (Ducey quickly backed down.)

If Kaepernick and Nike were under attack for criticizing police, who deserve every bit of it, then white America had exposed itself yet again in its willingness to sacrifice black life, in its complete and criminal lack of interest in justice. Neither of which, we all know at this late date, is the issue even closely approximating the real one: white people's desire for black people to be the quiet, obedient renters of the American dream. This unknowable percentage of Americans who believed these things and burned their own belongings could not be dismissed as an irrational or racist fringe because chief among their legions was the power: the president of the United States, police chiefs, local mayors, and state governors. This was what America was, and my mind had to change.

IT'S OK TO CRITICIZE THE MILITARY

Between 2009 and 2016, a period better known as the Obama presidency, the United States spent more money arming Saudi Arabia than during any previous presidential administration in history. This is the same Saudi Arabia with an atrocious human rights record, whose treatment of women, if it were any other country, would have been long ago been condemned with US sanctions. The same Saudi Arabia where, in 2018, *Washington Post* journalist Jamal Khashoggi was brutally murdered at the behest of the Saudi government. The US then talked really tough—but did next to nothing. The same Saudi Arabia of which fifteen of the nineteen hijackers responsible for carrying out the September 11, 2001, attacks were citizens. According to the Security Assistance Monitor, which catalogs US military and security assistance to other countries, the Obama administration authorized more than $115 billion in weapons sales to Saudi Arabia, and in turn, the Saudis used their status as a prime Pentagon weapons partner to engage in a ruthless assault on Yemen. While Barack Obama slowed weapons sales to the country with the intention of halting them completely, Donald Trump *increased* munition sales to the Saudis with the immoral justification that if the United States didn't arm Saudi Arabia, Russia or China certainly would.

In the years immediately following 9/11 under George W.

Bush, the United States authorized in excess of two hundred drone strikes against Yemen alone. The United States maintains more than two hundred nuclear warheads in Western Europe. The Costs of War Project at Brown University reports that from 9/11 through 2018, the United States waged war or maintained a military presence in seventy-six nations. That's 39 percent of the world's countries.

The militarization of post-9/11 America, known as the Global War on Terror, transformed American culture—whether the subject is sports or policing, Hollywood or media. Or fashion—such as camouflage jumpsuits, jackets, and yoga pants. Or travel. The high-end travel apparel firm Tumi sells $1,000 camouflage-patterned luggage. If the purpose of camouflage is to disguise itself in an environment, the military has succeeded in blending itself into every aspect of American life. The government's notorious 1033 program allows the Pentagon to transfer military equipment to civilian law enforcement, because if there's one thing your average local police department really needs, it's a mine-resistant tank.[1] The 1033 program remade the image of police departments across America, which now often resemble occupying forces instead of ostensibly vital allies of communities. It is Main Street as Fallujah, with police wearing the drab desert fatigues and manning Mine-Resistant Ambush Protected vehicles (MRAPs, if you're using the lingo)—*in America. Against American citizens.* Well, *some* American citizens.

State police maintain recruiting offices on military bases, allowing for discharged soldiers to take police exams, paving a smooth transition from warrior-soldier to warrior-cop. Genuflection toward the military is a requirement at sporting events, embedded through undisclosed financial relationships between military branches and teams, which is sold to the public as the NFL or NBA supporting "the troops." The military pays sports teams to promote war. The subservient public laps it up, and the dissenters are punished as un-American (and perhaps they are, for criticizing the earning of a dollar). Every day in America, the business of militarization masquerades as patriotism.[2]

There are many facets to the grotesqueness of Donald Trump's America, and his desperation to profit from militarization is certainly one of them. Blind militarism is the legacy of 9/11, not something caused by Trump, despite the panicked revisionism that Trump and Trump alone is the source of the country's pathologies. It isn't his America at all. Trump attempted to claim himself as the military's original champion by demanding an unquestioned loyalty and deference to it but its ubiquity in the culture is also not of his doing, even if he did spend the first year of his presidency unsuccessfully trying to garner support for a military parade worthy of a third-world despot, but finally succeeding in the embarrassment in his third. For all of his incompetence and crassness, Trump has provided convenient cover for the decades that preceded him, and his existence represents not a root but a culmination of decline obvious to anyone not actively engaged in the soothing ritual of avoidance. His particular level of grotesqueness has rehabilitated the thinkers, voters, and policymakers who predated him. Compared to him, they can reposition themselves to appear statesmanlike. They get to appear reasonable. They get to bask smugly in their reasonableness. They get to reshape their time into one when Good Americans believed in the oneness of the republic and simply had legitimate and respectful differences of opinion. Take, for example, the viral image of George W. Bush handing Michelle Obama a cough drop at John McCain's funeral. A kinder, simpler, bipartisan time. They get to appear benign. They are not. "No president since World War II has contributed more to the militarization of the United States than President Bush," wrote intelligence expert Melvin A. Goodman in 2013. "Under his leadership from 2001 to 2009, the United States fought two unsuccessful wars, experienced a financial crisis, initiated irreversible tax cuts that burden the US economy and compromised the rule of law at home and abroad. President Bush's militarization of foreign and national security policy included the creation of an entrenched national security state."[3]

The terrorizing of black citizens by the barrel of the peacemaker, the callous legislative siphoning of public resources, and the economic suffocation of citizens by financial institutions are now what they were then, exacerbated by Trump's demagoguery and hypernationalism but not created by them. The dismissal of dissenters as merely hysterical, hyperbolic, *dramatic* is the same response of yesteryear, with today containing a bit less remorse, a bit less lament, a bit less hope that the people on the top are trying to improve the lives of those on the bottom. Today there is no white man's burden. Today the power views itself as the victim. It may be therapeutic to assign the blame of this momentum to Trump, the elixir being his eventual removal from office, but this would be yet another exercise in magical thinking. It isn't all him. It never was.

With one enormous exception, issues face some form of public opposition. For the police, the Black Lives Matter movement voiced dissent. The #MeToo hashtags, pussy hats, congressional testimonies, and courageous first-person admissions of sexual assault victims exposed Trump and Brett Kavanaugh and Harvey Weinstein, and convicted Larry Nassar and Bill Cosby and an entire culture of powerful, predatory men. The March for Our Lives was a direct response, finally, to America's acceptance of mass shootings.

Twenty years of military war, waste, and blood, however, has produced a militarized state in priority, culture, and attitude. In 2012 and 2016, as well as the early stages of 2020, our endless war reflex isn't even a topic, never mind a priority. Congress doesn't even authorize use of force anymore. Presidents decide who to attack, when, and for how long. Americans in the shadow of 9/11 have surrendered a right that was once a given: it's OK to criticize the military. It is, in fact, a necessity.

RABBITS

If there's one certainty in America, it is that the military has created for itself a shield of invincibility. It is a shield, incidentally, made of cloth. It is the American flag.

The flag does not stand for values. It does not stand for freedom. It represents the military and loyalty to it. When there is resistance in this country, it better not be toward the military. When the military is involved, even the dissidents scurry like rabbits, falling in line as good Americans. When Colin Kaepernick took a knee, he made certain—doubly certain—that his protest did not include any criticism of the military. He did this even though police rolled through the black communities of Ferguson, Missouri, and Baltimore outfitted in tactical gear and equipped with tanks provided by the Army. Kaepernick was so careful to not offend American military sensibilities that he did something he did not need to do: he sought out the counsel of a veteran, the former Green Beret Nate Boyer, to discuss the "most respectful way" to protest injustice without offending the troops. When Bruce Maxwell, the Oakland A's catcher, took a knee in September 2017, he reiterated that he came from a military family and never meant any disrespect to the troops. It did neither of them any good.

In another time, Maxwell's and Kaepernick's awakenings—like the awakenings of Malcolm X and Martin Luther King Jr. and Jackie Robinson—could not have avoided the inclusion of pan-Africanism, which would have forced a direct critique of the American military, which has impressed itself heavily on the black and brown peoples of the world. Robinson, a supporter of both Richard Nixon and the Vietnam War, eventually concluded the war was wrong despite his early public disagreement with King's antiwar position. Any critique of the American racial system, such as that of the Black Panther Party for Self-Defense, ultimately would have collided with American capitalism and

American imperialism, both of which have historically been reinforced by American military might.

President Dwight D. Eisenhower's fear of a military-industrial complex, long realized in the half century since his death, in 1969, has been enhanced by sports, which involves some of the nation's most visible corporations. The NFL, the NBA, MLB, NASCAR, the NCAA, and the NHL, as well as business partners such as Nike, ESPN, NBC, CBS, and Fox, among others, enthusiastically sell war to the public. With its thirst to concoct heroes, sports has been the military's most reliable corporate ally in anaesthetizing the public. At a Minnesota Twins–Kansas City Royals game in 2019, the public address announcer asked the crowd to remove their caps and pay tribute to the armed forces with the singing of the national anthem. Military before country.

The embedded presence of the armed forces in sports is the legacy of September 11 but also a cynical public relations triumph, capitalizing on fear while shuttering any meaningful opposition to war, for even the most resolute war critic would rethink challenging seventy thousand people at a Dallas Cowboys game saluting an F-14 Tomcat flyover. Dutifully, corporations play along, muzzling the public through sheer marketing muscle. During the 2017 and 2018 baseball seasons, the cellphone service provider T-Mobile ran an ad campaign promoting military discounts for families, battering viewers with the words "ARE YOU WITH US?" in block letters on TV screens across America. Being a business partner in America's war machine also means that individual players considering joining an antiwar movement risk not only their reputations in a country where challenge is viewed as treasonous, but their employment as well. It is a silencing.

It is also a departure, for military service was once accompanied by the incentive of personal betterment, a pathway to college, higher education that would translate to a better opportunity at a prosperous civilian life. Army advertising once sold travel and skills to recruits. They would learn computers. They could become engineers. Now, the selling point is to serve and kill. During the 2018 Dodgers–Red Sox World Series, the Army ran an ad campaign showing soldiers racing block to block through a bombed-out foreign city. As the camera followed fighters firing off rounds, the ad resembled a first-person shooter video game trailer. As the explosives detonated, the slogan "WARRIORS WANTED" flashed in bright-yellow text across the screen. Military recruitment commercials from the 1980s focused on service as an opportunity to be better positioned in the job market. "Serve your country while serving yourself," as one TV spot urged. Today, America is only asking for killers. In return, it does not promote education but obedience, and the strategy backfired badly. In the spring of 2019 the Army launched a Memorial Day social media campaign on Twitter, asking, "How has serving impacted you?" The overwhelming response to the question detailed the devastating human toll of war. "I know more people that have committed suicide in my unit than have been killed when we were deployed," Brandon Neely, one of the posters, told the *New York Times*. A few weeks later, he posted on his Twitter account, "The darkness of PTSD is hard to explain to those who will never know it personally."

The Costs of War Project estimates war violence has claimed more than 370,000 lives directly and more than 800,000 indirectly, displacing 10.1 million persons worldwide. Through 2018, the project reports, America's Global War on Terror will produce a $5.6 *trillion*[4] price tag for American taxpayers and that does not factor in the effects of war on the environment— and no one is allowed or willing to discuss it.

"This is one big reason to link the military to sports, to distract us from the horrendous costs of war," retired Air Force Lieutenant Colonel William Astore told me. "To wrap these wars in the flag, to see support for them as 'patriotic,' we cheer on the troops like we cheer on our favorite athletes. Meanwhile, few Americans have any idea how much these wars are costing us, not only in money. They're weakening and corrupting the soul of our country: our ideals."

THE SMOTHERING EFFECT

In the wake of 9/11, the United States adopted ambitious security goals that extended the reach of American forces as the United States responded to perceived security challenges. A great part of the spending dealt with wars in Iraq (Operation Iraqi Freedom) and Afghanistan (Operation Enduring Freedom) that began with little congressional debate and virtually no public concern, let alone opposition.

—Melvin Goodman, *National Insecurity*[5]

There is no sustained antiwar movement in America, no challenge to or public debate about the direction in which the country has been taken. *Terrorism* has become the bipartisan blank check to fear the world, spend money beyond the reasonable on defense, and mute any thought that runs counter to the bulldozing narrative being shoved down every American's throat. There are layers of irony to this: Americans believe their flag is a symbol of freedom yet they are scared of the world. George W. Bush told Americans to shop in the wake of the 9/11 attacks yet is the person most responsible for turning the country into a land of walls and missiles and deference.

The grassroots fights but the upwardly mobile, the college educated, the upper middle class, the nonmarchers who once joined them because they couldn't take their kids being sacrificed to endless war anymore have traded their picket signs for car magnets. This section of America abandoned dissent because they haven't been fighting America's wars since the draft was dissolved in 1973. Their kids are safe. It is only the white poor, the black and brown without the connections to avoid it who are still the expendable ones, who must trade their bodies for the opportunity of an education without public outrage over the harm coming their way. There is little discussion in the discussion halls. George W. Bush fought two immoral wars. Barack Obama authorized force in Syria without congressional approval and extended the war in Afghanistan abroad and surveillance at home. It has been more than thirty years since the American people have elected a president who served in the military, and as civilian oversight of the armed forces—once an essential staple of governance—continues to wane, even elected officials are expected to kneel before the professional military class and do what they're told.

Meanwhile, corporate partners keep the public in line. From Nike to Lowe's to Home Depot to T-Mobile to the NFL, sports marketing is designed to stifle opinion by creating the illusion of pageantry and by offering the troops military discounts on all clothing and apparel. Pickup trucks are sold to the public using the term "made with military-grade materials." At the airport, active military gets to board first, and now hotel chains including Hyatt, Marriott, and Hilton offer military discounts. On Amtrak, a lead car on the Boston-to-Washington, DC, Acela Express is painted with a sign thanking the troops for their service. There was a time when America, at least in theory, was willing to accept the notion of hating war without hating the warrior, but today the culture only accepts support of the soldier through the support of the military—through silence, through obedience, and through twenty years of ribbons and car magnets and camouflage jerseys.

Smothered, the public cheers and the athletes are always very careful to remind everyone that whatever grievances they may have, they are *certainly not* criticizing the military. With their voices more powerful than ever, and the country drifting further from its recognizable principles, maybe they should.

"THIS IS NOT A WAY OF LIFE AT ALL."

During the campaign for the 2016 Democratic presidential nomination, Senator Bernie Sanders suggested the idea of "free college" for all Americans. It was a concept that sounded new and radical but the idea was nearly twice as old as Sanders. Americans of a certain generation remember hearing that for residents of the state, college tuition in California was "free." For nearly one hundred years, from 1868 to the mid-1960s, California did not charge its residents tuition. Tuition, along with higher fees, came about in 1966 only because of Governor Ronald Reagan's cuts to education funding. It was politics, not a lack of feasibility or imagination that killed the idea of free college. The notion that it was possible for a state to make higher education afford-able was not a theory but a program from which generations of students benefited. It wasn't fantasy. It *happened*.

The response to Sanders's proposal from the national news media—sarcasm, dismissal, disengagement with the idea—was predictable, intellectual sloth. The idea was treated as some form of amorphous futurism without historical precedent. It was as if Sanders had suggested colonizing Mars with free colleges. It was just Bernie doing his wacky Vermont socialist thing, tossing out ideas to seduce those young people that could not possibly work.

His opponent, Hillary Clinton, responded with the same knowing sarcasm, dismissal, and disengagement, but with an even more insulting conclusion: Sanders was being "unrealis-tic," a dreamy left-winger swept away by fantasy. He was not a Real Leader but a naïve political bumblebee, his nose buzz-ing in a coneflower. Free college sounded good but this wasn't the New Deal. It couldn't have been more anathema to the Way Things Are. Mature adults knew better, Clinton was say-ing, and by implication, rational voters should not take such reckless talk seriously. "I always remember what my late father said," Clinton said of Sanders's proposal, to applause from the ostensibly clear-thinking mainstream media. "If somebody offers you something for free, read the fine print."

What Clinton did not do—nor have the men who have occupied the White House—was acknowledge the truly unrealistic: financing endless war with money the country doesn't have. "Finally, these wars have been largely paid for by borrowing, part of the reason the US went from budget surplus to deficits after 2001," according to the Costs of War report. "Even if the US stopped spending on war at the end of this fiscal year, interest costs alone on borrowing to pay for the wars will continue to grow apace. . . . Future interest costs for overseas contingency operations spending alone are projected to add more than $1 trillion to the national debt by 2023. By 2056, a conservative estimate is that interest costs will be about $8 trillion unless the US changes the way it pays for the wars."[6]

It could also choose to fight fewer of them.

The mainstream piled on Sanders for being "unrealistic" (there's that word again) but Clinton's position was actively being undermined by a catastrophe occurring on the ground: the death of college as the gateway to the American dream. A 2017 College Board report stated that from 1987 and 2017, the price of attending a four-year public college rose by 213 percent. For private colleges, it was 129 percent.

While corporations across the country demand at least a bachelor's degree as the first hurdle to the joining the workforce and often a master's degree to more realistically compete, millions of Americans were being devastated by crushing student debt. According to *Forbes*, 44 million borrowers in 2016 owed a total of $1.52 trillion in student debt. In 2019, according to the Institute for College Access and Success, the average student leaves college with $28,000 of debt.

More than 10 percent of those borrowers, totaling a staggering $31 billion, were at least ninety days delinquent on their loan payments. Twelve and a half million Americans, according to the magazine, owed student debt between $10,000 and $25,000, and the climbers—the key age demographic of thirty to thirty-nine, who are supposed to be purchasing houses, raising children, and seeing their earnings rise—were not climbing but drowning. Student debt for that group ballooned 30 percent in five years.

When America loses, black people are devastated, for the numbers inside of the numbers are crushing. Over a twelve-year period between 2004 and 2016, nearly half of African American students default on their student loans and nearly 70 percent drop out of college, compared to 21 percent and 38 percent, respectively, for white students, according to 2017 federal data. Seton Hall assistant professor Robert Kelchen reported that, in 2016, 30 percent of African American graduate students carried at least $100,000 in debt.

Free college is now a core issue in the 2020 election cycle, but only with slightly more legitimacy, worthy of discussion but still framed as dreamy, financially unfeasible, a socialist handout to deadbeats and, most importantly, completely uncoupled to the rising, runaway defense budget.

As the policymakers, pundits, and presidential candidates told anyone who believed a different, better way was possible to shut up and be realistic because this is How Things Are, Americans were going backward, blaming millennials for eating too much avocado toast.

The numbers were staggering. According to a 2017 Census report, 26 percent of Americans ages eighteen to thirty-four lived with their parents in 2005. By 2015, that number had risen to 34.1 percent. Meanwhile, the government passed defense-spending budgets of $523 billion (2016), $639 billion (2017), and $717 billion (2018). That $717 billion came at the expense of a 13 percent cut in federal education spending and comprised nearly 56 percent of all federal spending. In the early 1950s, when President Eisenhower worried that Cold War military spending escalations with the Soviet Union threatened to turn the US into a "Garrison State," federal spending on defense had reached 50 percent.

"This world in arms is not spending money alone. It is spending the seat of its laborers, the genius of its scientists, the hopes of its children. The cost of one modern heavy bomber is this: a modern brick school in more than thirty cities. It is two electric power plants, each serving a town of 60,000 population," Eisenhower said in 1953. "We pay for a single fighter with a half-million bushels of wheat. We pay for a single destroyer with new homes that could have housed more than 8,000 people. . . . This is not a way of life at all, in any true sense. Under the cloud of threatening war, it is humanity hanging from a cross of iron."[7]

Sixty-three years later it was particularly galling to be told to be realistic under the shadow of staggering debt; suppression of criticizing the surging US war machine under the threat of being labeled unpatriotic; and the notion that accepting that the United States manufactures missiles that are sold to Saudi Arabia and kill Yeminis is somehow an example of maturity. Equally galling was the premise that spending nearly three quarters of a trillion dollars on the military is disconnected from making spending in other areas possible, such as on making college affordable on a large scale or improving drinking water, health care, or infrastructure. Most galling is being told not to question a five-to-one ratio of spending on defense over education while the debts pile ever higher, lest one be branded disloyal to the country and "disrespectful to the troops." Criticizing the military is especially essential when discretionary spending for the armed forces is four times that of spending on the veterans Americans have conveniently used as a shield to smother dissent. If there is a certainty to American life, where according to the Department of Agriculture the United States wastes nearly 50 percent of the food it produces, where $6.5 billion was spent on the 2016 elections alone, where the New York City subway system is crumbling but the Giuliani administration gifted more than $3 billion to the New York Mets and New York Yankees for two new baseball-only stadiums, where somehow broke cities across the country seem to have endless budgets to pay out police brutality settlements, it is this: there is currently plenty of money in the nation.

Eventually, in the November general election, Hillary Clinton received my vote for president. In the Massachusetts primary, largely because of her attitude on this question, she did not. I did not appreciate being told by someone asking me for my support to grow up and think realistically. I preferred being told that endless spending for endless killing was far more unrealistic and that it was possible for the nation to adopt a worldview that to me was not unreasonable but preferable.* I preferred a leader who could offer a glimpse of what was possible instead of treating me like a flaky dreamer who first wanted free college and then maybe a pony.

---

* Apparently, neither did Clinton, who, in July 2016, after receiving the Democratic nomination, adopted her own version of Sanders's tuition proposal. "It's imperative the next president put forward a bold plan to make debt-free college available to all," her campaign statement read. "My New College Compact will do just that—by making sure working families can send a child or loved one to college tuition-free and by giving student-debt holders immediate relief."

COPAGANDA

Periodically and without warning I will ask friends a question: "Have you ever murdered anyone, and if not, why?" It is not a trick question but indeed a serious one. Initially, respondents lean toward deterrent to explain why they haven't. "Because," they will say, "I don't want to go to jail." Upon reflection, most people voluntarily correct course, rediscover their humanity, and offer some variant of "Because I have no desire to murder anyone." The same is true, they will also say, of their lack of desire to steal, assault, rape, kidnap, burglarize, or engage in virtually any other type of crime.

America prefers to view itself as a civilized society and, as such, the latter is the obvious, proper, and *decent* response. Yet judging by its obsession with law enforcement, America acts as if the former is its natural order—that violent crime is but a bad mood away and only the shield, the Glock, and the squad car stand between life and senseless death at the hands of our neighbors. Americans cling to this contrived state of emergency despite decades of research confirming that killing as a primary instinct is extremely rare, a dystopian fantasy compared to the socioeconomic factors that drive people to violent crime. Despite a spike in mass shootings, the actual murder rate was roughly the same in 2018 as it was in 1960, according to crime statistics compiled by the *New York Times*. That most people have no desire to harm others is also, and should always be, *unsurprising*.

Where I live, a bumper sticker commonly seen around town reads "Troopers Are Your Best Protection." It is a specious declaration at best, at worst a cynical attempt to advance the political and economic agendas that come with commodifying law enforcement and the criminal justice system. If data mean anything, prosperity and opportunity, not police, are one's best protection—yet law enforcement in America is omnipresent. Police are a fixture of the national identity, central to its popular culture and, in post-9/11 America, under the guise of freedom and safety, are emboldened to only further increase their footprint. The land of the free feels occupied by the smothering, militarized presence of police. Police are encouraged—by media-manipulated juries, by a decades-long unaccountability, by supplicant, politicized judges, and, of course, by fear—to ignore or break the law while judges and legislatures endorse propolice, antidemocratic policies. All, presumably, to keep us safe. Though charged with completely different responsibilities, in order to further exploit the fear, police attempt to make themselves indistinguishable from the military, try to look like domestic agents in the War on Terror. As a public relations tactic they have taken a dangerous, divisive job and rebranded it under the reassuring, unimpeachable post-9/11 umbrella of a single, uncomplicated word: *heroes*.

The public receives these maneuverings with pride. An overpoliced America—in schools, on TV, in train stations, at ballparks—is not considered by the mainstream to be a chilling harbinger of authoritarianism but a source of strength. No other occupation in the country owns as wide a gap between its realities and its public packaging as law enforcement because quite possibly no other occupation owns such distance between its experiences with different slices of the public. For those who are white and middle-class, the police are part of the social fabric, an unquestioned ally. The image of the police diverges almost exclusively along racial and class lines. The white mainstream accepts an image of benevolence, fairness, and *justice* while those who are black, brown, and poor know firsthand that the police are *possibly* all of those things but also *definitely* can be brutal, oppressive, merciless, aggressive, and extralegal. As a defense against criticism and a ploy for bigger budgets and more presence, police departments around the country routinely sell more fear and maintain that ungrateful American citizens are at war with them. If it is true that no occupation in America enjoys as great a distance between fantasy and reality as law enforcement, it is also true that none has spent so much time and money constructing such an illusion of itself. Nor has any other benefited from the assistance of so many powerful enablers—in Hollywood, in the newsrooms, and now at the ballparks—who are invested in sustaining their illusion. There are, indeed, so many ways to tell a lie. Police propaganda may well be America's favorite.

PRODUCT PLACEMENT

"The thing which we are all up against is propaganda," the journalist Dorothy Thompson said in a 1935 address to the American Society of Newspaper Editors. "Sometimes I think that this age is going to be called the age of propaganda, an unprecedented rise of propaganda, propaganda as a weapon, propaganda as a technique, propaganda as a fine art, and propaganda as a form of government."

At Fenway Park, for all eighty-one Red Sox home games, a member of the Boston Police Department sits in the dugout. Right next to the players. Another stands in the bullpen. In between innings at Yankee Stadium, more than a half-dozen police officers—not grounds crew or stadium security—ring the field. During an NBA game, a police officer is often stationed in a row directly behind each coach. During timeouts, police guard the court as well. At the end of every football game, pro or college, the two head coaches jog out to midfield to shake hands, each flanked by police officers. None of this is a coincidence. Nor, it should be noted, is it by accident that these officers are virtually always in direct view of television cameras, reinforcing their presence to the audience dozens of times per night. It's a constant reminder of the ubiquitous threat—even a relief pitcher might be in danger. The messaging is about as subtle as pornography: troopers are your best protection.

During the 2018 season Major League Baseball teams hosted nearly fifty "Law Enforcement Appreciation" nights in stadiums around the country. The NBA, NHL, and NFL do the same, staging some form of "Heroes" acknowledgment between periods, demanding that tens of thousands of paying customers thank police. Across the major sports, where the public looks harshly at black athletes and says it wants sports and only sports and none of life's political or social complications, more than one hundred nights a year—nearly a third of every calendar year—are dedicated to honoring law enforcement. Police are not only honored as heroes but, like the military, receive ticket discounts from every sports team in America. These discounts are not available to nurses or schoolteachers or mental health professionals but to people with guns, and sometimes the catchall of "first responders," which sometimes includes firefighters and EMTs. Discounted tickets are available to police for NCAA games, Disney theme parks, hotels, Broadway theater tickets, and hundreds of other products and services. The sneaker company Reebok offers a 20 percent "Heroes discount" to law enforcement.

Two weeks before Christmas 2018 the website dealhack.com published the Dealhack First Responder Discount List—in their words, "a quarterly survey of brands that offer discounts to first responders." From eyewear to hotels, sports to housing, insurance to travel and cars, the website listed the 165 companies that offer the sweetest deals to the cops, a thank you for their service. Once one peels back the layers, the harsh reaction to Colin Kaepernick becomes clearer. He wasn't just supporting black people. He was challenging the monetizing of the cop/corporate state.

On December 10, 2018, the Hollywood trade website Deadline.com reported that NBC had begun development on *Conway*, a new crime drama about a detective who wakes from a coma and finds he has "exceptional cognitive abilities." The headline, "Vin Diesel to Produce Cop Drama 'Conway' in Works at NBC," continued a tradition of police-as-entertainment that dates to the earliest days of television, perfected now by the glutting of cop dramas, cop buddy movies, and cop faux documentaries. Now, cops are superheroes. Several early shows of the 1960s, such as *The FBI* and *Dragnet*, like the later *Cops*, were written, funded, and controlled by active law enforcement. *The FBI* was created as a recruitment tool for the bureau and also a powerful vehicle to improve the FBI's public image while it secretly infiltrated organizations and surveilled and killed American citizens. As racial tensions rose during the 1960s, *Dragnet* projected a clean-cut alternative to the skull-cracking reputation that the Los Angeles Police Department owned in the black community. The *Washington Post* described the show's relationship with the notoriously racist LAPD chief William Parker and with department "publicity wizard" Stanley Sheldon as "accepting stringent censorship from the police department in exchange for story ideas, logistical help, and a patina of truth. That bargain would help create America's first enduring cop drama and a model for police storytelling for decades to come."

That bargain created the template. An industry followed. A 2016 Oxford Research Encyclopedia report stated that more than three hundred police dramas have aired on American television since 1950. The police, living in the background in other Western countries, are principal actors in America, with film and television being used to win over the public, burnish law enforcement's reputation, and align dissent with criminality. Whoever the heroic police fought on the screen—pimps, pushers, murderers, black nationalists, antiwar protesters—were the villains to the public sitting on their couches across America.

Invariably, the sustainable villain is black, and as black people began to ask for things, the more villainous they would become. The more visible black people became in the real world, so, too, did law enforcement become more visible in the new medium. The two went hand in hand. The police became a television colossus, financially and culturally. The black people did not receive royalties.

It is money well spent. The embedding of police not as a neutral force, not as an unfortunate necessity, but as a *force for good* permeates not only pop culture but real life in America. Being the friend, the confidant, the basketball coach, the problem solver on screen affords them the inherited, positive characteristics that protect law enforcement from its own real-life misconduct, its racism, its corruption, and its murders. The police owe their reputation not nearly as much to good works as to a nearly three-quarters-of-a-century-long public relations machine played out over the airwaves. Their rehabilitation is a priority, protection of their reputation a must. "Whereas police are humanized through the use of actual names and portrayed as courageous defenders against the hordes of the criminally insane, the voice of the citizen-suspect is given little credibility," reported a 2004 study in the *Western Journal of Communication* on the long-running television show *Cops*. "In *Cops*, requests for clarification of the reasons for stops are dismissed and met with increasing aggression by police."

None of this would carry much importance if the public were able to relegate what they see of police on the screen to the realm of entertainment, but studies of the effect of flooding the airwaves with police dramas show that large numbers of Americans shape their image of law enforcement from television, whether notorious reality shows like *Cops* or clear fictional dramas such as *Law and Order*. Studies reveal not only that Americans often form favorable opinions of police from television but also that cop shows are where they learn how police departments function. "It's the best recruitment tool for policing ever," Randy Sutton, a retired Las Vegas police officer, said about *Cops*. The *Western Journal of Communication* study on reality-based police dramas concluded that "even as violent crime rates decline, these programs may encourage fear by over-representing violent crime. By promoting a fear of crime and the image that minorities are responsible for most crime, these reality programs may serve as justification for harsher penalties and even police aggression toward citizen-suspects."

Television conditions Americans to accept wide ranges of force used against suspects. It is a symptom more than a cause, of course, because this deadly farce is not merely the result of cop buddy movies. The numbers reinforce the attitudes that play out every day, on juries, at parties, over dinner: the child-ish need for justice to be uncomplicated. A study appearing in the 2015 issue of *Criminal Justice and Behavior* on the effect of police dramas on the public reported that only one in ten re-spondents believed police used force when making an arrest, but when police did, 79 percent believed the suspect "deserved it." The study also reported that 63 percent of respondents believe police "rarely or never" coerced false confessions from subjects. The study concluded that "watching crime dramas increases the probability of believing the use of force was necessary by six percentage points." They're living in fantasy.

Meanwhile, in real life, the numbers shatter families. The *Washington Post* reported 995 people were killed by police in 2015, 963 in 2016, and 987 in 2017. That's 2,945 people in three years. Those years saw videotaped recording of police killing Daniel Shaver, Terence Crutcher, Philando Castile, and Alton Sterling—with police being acquitted of wrongdoing in each case. On April 11, 2015, the *Washington Post* reported, "Among the thousands of fatal shootings at the hands of police since 2005, only 54 officers have been charged." A June 2018 Gallup poll concluded that 54 percent of respondents reported a "great deal" or "quite a lot" of confidence in police, third be-hind the military (74 percent) and small business (67 percent).

None of the next twelve categories garnered even 40 percent confidence. The American Bar Association reported twenty-nine wrongful-conviction rulings in 2017 involving police extracting false confessions. It's a small number—unless you happen to be one of them.

HEROES

A few weeks before dealhack.com listed the companies offering the best police discounts, four St. Louis Police Department officers were indicted for beating a protester during a demonstration a year earlier. The protester was black and defenseless and, according to FBI investigators, complied with officers' commands before they threw him to the ground and beat him with their nightsticks. One officer kicked him in the face, swelling his jaw so severely he could not eat for weeks. The man suffered a two-centimeter hole in his face from the beating, which was described in the police report as a "cut on the lip." In text messages, the officers bragged about illegally beating protesters, with the added bonus of being able to do so without fear of being recognized because their riot gear did not include their names. "It's gonna be a lot of fun beating the hell out of these shitheads once the sun goes down and nobody can tell us apart," one text read. Afterward, another texted, "It was a blast beating people that deserve it." They were cops. They could abuse citizens and they knew it. They were heroes. In 2016, Gallup reported 80 percent of white respondents surveyed said they had a "great deal" of respect for police in their area. One of the officers involved in the beating texted another to make sure "an old white guy" was present whenever they beat a protester. Old white guys always trust the police, they knew. The three officers were indicted for their assault. A fourth, another officer who was in a relationship with one of the assailants, was indicted for lying to investigators, and all four were indicted on another count of covering up the assault.

It is possible, probable even, that the officers would have

gotten away with all of it and none of the charges would have been levied if not for the fantastical appearance of bad luck—Hollywood-movie level, Sidney Poitier in *In the Heat of the Night*–level bad luck—for the cops. The black man they pummeled happened not to be some faceless, rightsless nobody of another untrustworthy black man but instead was the St. Louis PD's own Luther Hall, a twenty-two-year veteran of the force who happened to be working the crowd on an undercover assignment. The alt-weekly *Riverfront Times* reported that Hall told investigators his fellow officers "beat the fuck out of him like Rodney King."

On September 15, 2018, eight thousand Massachusetts residents were affected by a gas emergency that set off explosions and cut off power in sections of the northeastern part of the state. Using a computer screenshot, state police posted a map to Twitter of the affected areas, warning residents to evacuate at the smell of gas. The screenshot included, inadvertently, a bookmark of several organizations, all of which were politically left, one of which—Mass Action Against Police Brutality—was directly committed to police reform. Less than thirty minutes later the post was deleted but it was too late. The Massachusetts State Police, notoriously secretive and already under investigation by the state for fraud, attempting to destroy payroll records, and other infractions, had tipped their hand: they were spying on left-wing groups under a program that monitors and collects information "relevant to terrorism and public safety." This at a time when even the FBI was on record confirming the alarming rise of white nationalist groups in the country. The *New York Times*, laughably if not for the gravity of the insult, even published a lengthy story on November 3, 2018, detailing how, amid stoking by the Trump White House, law enforcement "failed to see the threat of white nationalism." The Twitter gaffe explained it: the cops were surveilling the wrong people.

Three weeks after the *Times* piece, the Northern California chapter of the American Civil Liberties Union filed a suit against the San Francisco Police Department for racially profiling black citizens during undercover drug arrests. The SFPD had had its own text-messaging scandal involving its bias against black citizens in 2011 and 2012, when white police officers joked about "burning crosses" and called biracial children "half-breeds" who were "an abomination of nature." Earlier in the 2018 season, on July 26, the San Francisco Giants held Law Enforcement Appreciation Night.

The list of similar actions by police across the country is virtually endless, whether it is based on a calendar year or a century, from Jackie Robinson testifying to Congress in 1949 about the reality of police brutality in black communities; to the oppressive tactics that led to the formation of the Black Panther Party in the 1960s; to the Abner Louima and Amadou Diallo cases in New York in the 1990s; to high-profile shootings in the Black Lives Matter era such as Chicago Police shooting seventeen-year-old Laquan McDonald sixteen times; to racial profiling by police, whether in St. Louis or San Francisco or Boston. After killing unarmed, unthreatening, and sobbing Daniel Shaver, fired Mesa, Arizona, police officer Philip Brailsford appealed to receive a pension under a PTSD medical claim. The claim was approved in July 2019; Brailsford was rehired and his firing rescinded. Under the terms of his pension, the city of Mesa agreed to pay the twenty-eight-year-old Brailsford $31,000 per year for the rest of his life, provide a job reference of "neutral," while covering up to $3 million for any potential legal fees or civil settlements filed against him for killing Shaver. If justice were real, Philip Brailsford would be a murderer as well as a killer, and if he lives to the average male life expectancy of seventy-eight, the state will have paid him $2.5 million, but no amount of body-cam videos or racist text messages or egregious payout settlements shifts the attitude toward police that the mainstream clings to with a childlike fidelity. Policing in America is not an occupation. It is an ideal.

THE GLUE OF WHITENESS

What, it must be wondered, is so valuable that these truths, fatal to virtually any other profession, are tolerated, protected, and justified when exposed regarding police? Nearly three thousand killings by police over a three-year period—several of unarmed citizens and captured on video—with a less than virtually non-existent conviction rate of officers. Evidence that policemen are often aligned with white nationalist organizations. False confessions. Fraud. Illegal surveillance. Billions paid out in civil settlements. The National Center for Women and Policing reported in 2014 that 10 percent of American families experience domestic violence, but for police officers' families, the number is two to four times higher, one of the highest rates in the nation, though given the issue's national coverage a first guess would be that the highest rate involves black football players. Though steroids are largely associated with sports, there is a culture of anabolic steroid use among police, as documented in University of Texas professor John M. Hoberman's searing book *Dopers in Uniform*.

This is the evidence, not conjecture or theory, of an institution facing enormous challenges, one in desperate need of reform and oversight. The reality repudiates the public relations. The transgressions, as widespread as they are disparate, explain at least in part the existence of the propaganda, for actual police-work is neither clean nor often heroic. After an officer with the Cleveland Police Department killed twelve-year-old Tamir Rice within two seconds of encountering him in 2014, the department paid his family a $6 million settlement of taxpayer money (without admitting wrongdoing, of course) and then publicly and shamelessly said the family should donate the money to charity. Killing a child, then painting the survivors as greedy lottery winners, isn't quite the appropriate selling point for Cleveland Indians Law Enforcement Appreciation Night.

In April 2019, *USA Today* reported that over the previous decade, eighty-five thousand police officers had been investigated or disciplined for misconduct. "Officers have beaten members of the public, planted evidence and used their badges to harass women," the report read. "They have lied, stolen, dealt drugs, driven drunk and abused their spouses." The report documented more than two thousand examples of "perjury, tampering with evidence or falsifying reports." Twenty officers were the subject of at least one hundred allegations each but remained on the job.

It is not simply power that prevents the public and the corporate machine from challenging law enforcement. (The Catholic Church was an equally if not even more powerful institution and yet has not recovered from its breaking of the public trust and quite likely never will.) The critical difference, beyond the one-liners-and-ammo formula of Hollywood cop-buddy movies, beyond the Blue Lives Matter police union intimidation, and beyond all the post-9/11 hero talk, is what the idea of law enforcement means to white mainstream culture. Policing is the glue of whiteness. Like the white American identity, which has never reconciled with the bloody and murderous roots of its empire, the police propaganda smothering the culture asserts an inherent goodness. Police are good, even when they kill, even when they break or flout the law, even when they roll tanks into Ferguson or occupy minority communities dressed as if they are invading Aleppo, which makes their transgressions forgivable. The same is true of whiteness, when it first appeared on the shores of a brown nation, when it isolates and then displaces to gentrify, when it annexes land, appropriates resources, and colonizes and then leads humanitarian efforts. Its presence must always be concluded to be a positive one. The myth of police as essential to goodness and not to whiteness must be protected as vigilantly as one protects the flag. For if it is not, and law enforcement, justice and whiteness are coupled, as the black and the brown know they always have been, then neutrality crumbles. The government, the law, the Constitution, and the commitment to equality are no longer objective and they must then be seen as the black person sees them—as the enforcement arm of whiteness. Heroism falls apart. The entire idea must be reconstituted.

Conversely, if police allow themselves to be the enforcement arm of whiteness, then who is the natural target, the obvious threat? It is the nonwhite. Black people have found themselves the targets of a particular phenomenon: white people (white women primarily) across the country calling the police on them. Whether it's a white woman calling police on a black female student napping in the Yale library, an employee calling police on two black friends awaiting another at a Starbucks in Philadelphia, or a white woman phoning police on a black family barbecuing in an Oakland park, the message is that black people do not belong in public spaces. When they are in public they are being watched not only by police but by average citizens who have chosen to aid in the policing. In 2019, a woman photographed a black Washington, DC, transit worker eating on the Metro, taking the time to tweet her bosses demanding the woman be disciplined.

Black presence suggests threat and becomes an unintended consequence of the War on Terror's "If you see something, say something" mandate. Taking this slogan to its natural conclusion, if the public is enlisted as agents of the state, their actions will reflect their fears, and their fear is black people. If the public does not believe black people belong in common, everyday American spaces without tight monitoring, then black people, like the Boston Marathon bombers or ISIS sympathizers, become the threat. The police become the personal protectors of the white public. They will be asked and expected to remove black people from spaces that white people do not believe African Americans have a right to share.

Calling the police on black people is an extension of the public and police's willingness to believe in black criminality, which has long been used by white perpetrators of heinous crime. In 1990, Charles Stuart infamously murdered his pregnant wife in Boston and blamed it on a black male. In 1995, Susan Smith drowned her two children and told police a black man killed her children after a carjacking. Two weeks before the 2008 election a twenty-year-old John McCain campaign volunteer named Ashley Todd claimed a black Obama supporter had attacked her and scratched the letter "B" into her face. In each case, law enforcement acted as the perpetrators had hoped, rounding up black suspects, quick to believe in black malfeasance as credible. Black people were used as the bait by the white perpetrators for one reason: they knew that at a first glance, and sometimes a first glance is all it takes, it would work. Existing while black.

Yet within this dynamic, when white people believe the law is designed to protect only them, and when they know they can act upon this belief at will, brazenly dialing 911 whenever they feel a black person has forgotten his or her place, the idea of white benevolence disintegrates as quickly as the neutrality of law enforcement. Whites can view themselves as both the conqueror and the asset that must be protected. Police are the occupiers, ready at a moment's notice to enforce the will not of justice for all but of whiteness.

Without the pretense of fairness, the nostalgia of the self-made fantasy, of police pulling themselves up and out of the lower class through the virtue of aiding justice becomes, finally and inevitably, ridiculous. Police is so tied to whiteness because it was the pathway to the American dream. Law enforcement provided one of the earliest opportunities for so many whites, especially big-city Italians, Poles, and Irish, to rise from immigrant to American. The blue-collar police and fire departments represented their path to legitimacy, to assimilation, built their middle class. It is how the Irish graduated from disorderly to white to hero. It is how the Italians transformed from criminal to white to hero. Just as with the military, there is nostalgia in the dynastic qualities of law enforcement, of how the son followed the father who followed his father into the business, the myth of gallantry maintained, that a valuable and noble trek from the Old World to the New was being completed.

It is a story darkly revived in post-9/11 America, except the inherent goodness of police transformed from the old Officer Friendly archetype into that of vigilant superpatriot. The former offered the melting pot a chance that community belonged to all people. The latter is a snarling defense of whiteness, patriotism, and xenophobia so deeply embedded into the culture that law enforcement now is cultivated as a patriotic business partner with professional sports leagues. One must ask: If Colin Kaepernick had taken a knee for global warming or education reform, would his industry and his country have lashed out so ferociously, so permanently?

Telling a different tale—that the Irish and Italian cops in Boston and New York, Philadelphia and Baltimore (not to mention Chicago and San Francisco), joined the American middle class by beating niggers over the head, by maintaining economic dominance over them through graft, corruption, and prohibiting them from joining police and fire departments in large numbers, only to come home and beat their spouses—would not spawn many enthusiastic TV shows. If the heroes weren't heroes, the nostalgic, self-made-immigrant story dissolves and the badge loses its appeal and becomes, as it has been for black people all along, something to fear.

UNRAVELING

Consider, then, what deconstruction of the police and its TV/movie/ballpark propaganda machine would do for black people. It would humanize them while indicting the untold hours of cop programming. It would mean that black people weren't lying after all. So many people, even without attending funerals or having their applications to the police academy rejected, have always known this to be untrue, that the stories of the Old World peasant arriving at Ellis Island with two dollars and a dream still placed them miles ahead of the richest black person because their impediments were not forever statutory. A pathway to becoming American existed, gave the immigrants hope. It gave them life. All they needed to do was work hard.

How, one wonders, now that there are black people, too, who can move to the suburbs, who can become cops, who can join the hero story as long as they stick to the script, has the space between us remained? We, those integrated members of the middle class, grew up side by side with our white friends in the same economic climates, our parents earning roughly the same money, trafficking ostensibly in the same postracial world. We saw the same viral videos and relied on each other's assumed decency, and, while watching the latest dashcam videos of another citizen shot unnecessarily by police, shared the same outrages. We thought we did.

Yet after the beers are cracked and another log gets tossed onto the fire and the subject turns to policing, not the horror of the black teen getting shot but *what to do about it and who is actually responsible*, the gaps grow wide and the silences long and the good white friends, the allies, will make nervous, bold jokes about how the police treat black people and how ridiculous and stupid Barbecue Becky was for calling the cops on black people. It is their nod to their black friends that they're in on it, that they get it and are among the good ones equally horrified by Walter Scott being gunned down by Michael Slager in South Carolina. Yet "getting it" and doing nothing to stop it is not much help to anyone.

Besides, everyone, in their own way, is "in on it," including the black people who give their own frustrated nod to the stories of driving while black but don't quite believe they are actually the target, not because they believe they are immune but because they, too, know fear, are sick of black kids doing stupid shit, scared of guns and crime, and when they're scared they believe that troopers, and not improved economic conditions, are their best protection. They, too, want to buy in to the power of the police state. It is how delusions thrive. No entity is more "in on it," of course, than the police themselves—the responsible ones who say just enough to sound reasonable and do just enough to thwart any hint of reform and who maintain solidarity with the rest of the force that threatens to withhold services because Beyoncé criticized police in a song or several Cleveland Browns once took a knee because the cops killed Tamir Rice. The people, the ones who are living under the increasingly occupying hostility of police, the ones who know firsthand the parts of the job—the ticketing quotas, the stop-and-frisk harassment, the revenue-generation imperatives, the text-message snickering about beating niggers over the head and getting away with it—that are never shown in the movies or on *Blue Bloods*, *CSI*, or *Hawaii Five-O* or mentioned during the Houston Astros Law Enforcement Appreciation Night, also knew something else from the hero worship post-9/11: their nightmare continued, increased, for the police were even more brazen now that they were no longer considered blue-collar city employees but the first line of the national domestic defense. The police even wear camouflage now, *desert* camo. In the middle of an American city. If there is a military-industrial complex, and surely there is, there exists also a police-industrial complex, and it demands obedience. All of this is necessary, we are told, to keep us safe. There are, as the feminist writer Rebecca Solnit wrote, many ways to tell a lie, and one of the best ways is to entertain the people who are listening to it.

2. POTEA

THE LOST TRIBE OF INTEGRATION

Seldom in my life have I lived in a neighborhood that was populated by a majority of black people. Dorchester was the first, when I was a kid, and it was so deeply segregated that newcomers to Boston didn't immediately realize blacks and whites were talking about the same place. Even though the streets run parallel to each other and are separated by less than a mile and a half, Dorchester Avenue—"Dot Ave.," as it is called—was theirs and Blue Hill Ave. was ours. Anyone referring to Dorchester as "Dot" has a ninety-nine and forty-four one hundredths percent chance of being white.

On the black side of Dorchester—the Blue Hill Ave. side—the only white people we saw were official or semi-official people: cops, firefighters, teachers, bill collectors, meter readers, shop owners, the physicians and dentists working at the free clinic across from Franklin Field. Unlike in neighboring Mattapan, there were no ethnic white holdouts from before the postwar migration, before the Jewish-German-Ukrainian neighborhoods turned black with the legal help from the banks and the real estate industry. The Dorchester of my childhood was black and brown.

There was much to remember: the street hockey where the black kids wanted to be Bobby Orr and the baseball in the vacant lot on the corner of Lucerne and Callender, where the lefthanded black kids wanted to be Yaz, and the pitchers con-torted themselves to look like Tiant; the Puerto Ricans across the street from our triple-decker and the Brazilians next door, the ones who drove a Volkswagen Thing and once kicked a soccer ball so hard it nearly broke my hand; the annual Franklin Park Kite Festival; the fire that burned down the house next to ours; the dead-ass vacant lot on Arbutus diagonal from our house the white surveyors would tell us when they came by the city was planning on turning into a swimming pool. (Spoiler alert: it never happened.)

There was also the running, speed produced by fear, try-ing not to panic. Concentrate on the footsteps. Don't panic. Panic slowed you down. Panic got you caught. The closer to the Franklin Field projects, the tougher the neighborhood. Floyd Street was the demarcating line, where friends lived and the games were played, but venturing above it, to Stratton and be-yond, that was dangerous. It got safer below Floyd. Home was close. Run down Lucerne on to Callender, cut across the vacant lot that used to be the *other* house that burned down, on to Ashton, into the house, where it was safe. *Don't* go past Arbutus on Halloween because the roughnecks were over there. I was probably seven or eight years old the time I went past Arbutus, not heeding the warnings, Icarus flying too close to the sun. An older kid approached me that night, told me how much he liked my costume, and then stole my candy.

Even at that age, a deal was being made with violence, like when my mother and father and sister celebrated the day I stopped running and turned and punched one of my tormenters dead in his fucking face. They cheered when you stopped run-ning because they knew if you did not stop running then, you'd be running for the rest of your life. You'd be running from them. You'd be running in the streets, in the classroom, and in the boardroom, and because you never stood up for yourself and no one would ever fear that you might one day turn and punch them dead in their fucking face. And then they would never stop chasing you. You'd be the mark. Punching back was the only way not to be the mark.

They cheered, because the ones who loved you and knew that they could not protect you every second now knew that you could be trusted to live. You now possessed the requisites to save your own life. They would tell that story with pride—about how you ran and ran, lured them past the front door, into the hallway and then—*bam!*—well into your adulthood. But *you* knew the difference: maybe they would stop chasing you, perhaps even be your friend since now you had passed the test and showed you were willing to throw a punch. Or maybe that day of triumph would produce different days of challenge, and maybe on the next challenge you would not win, like the time your older sister, who never lost, who beat anyone who messed with her little brother, lost. Ended up in the hospital. Nothing big, just a tetanus shot after one of the girls jumped her, ripping an earring clean out of her ear. They may have cheered the day I won, and they told the aunts and uncles, but they also recognized their children were now involved in a cycle of fighting, and as they aged, that fighting would graduate from fists to knives and guns, and maybe their kid would be Troy, the kid who lived on the corner of Floyd and Lucerne, got stabbed by Franklin Field when some kids tried to punk him for his summer-job money. He ran home scared, past the fire department on Blue Hill Ave. that could have saved his life, and bled to death on his front porch. They knew it, and that, combined with the growing conviction that receiving a quality education in Boston was becoming an impossibility, was why we left town.

"How does it feel to be a problem?" W. E. B. Du Bois famously wrote in 1902. The migration of blacks from the South has always brought with it a violent response: the riotous year of 1919, and several more following. The postwar migration years came with white flight; oppressive, legal, racially restrictive real estate covenants; blockbusting and redlining that maintained white communities; and the extralegal violence that accompanied school desegregation. The violence, it should be noted, occurred during and following world wars, where black soldiers volunteered to fight for what they wanted to believe was their country, too. Play with the words. Do the mental gymnastics, run from it all. Say it isn't what it is. Call it *heritage not hate* in defense of traitorous Confederate symbols in the South or *forced busing* and *self-determination* because white people don't want their kids sharing with black people in the North. Don't call it *racist*, but the end result is the same: when black people come, white people go, but before they go, they fight, both with their ballots and with their fists. And when they go they take their wealth with them, leaving behind a community in which financial institutions will not invest. The collusion between white flight and redlining is the foundational blocks of a slum.

"Whether whites are willing to remain in neighborhoods as they become more racially mixed is a second important part of the picture," reported a 2000 study of Boston housing patterns. "Few whites said they would move if Hispanics or Asians moved into the neighborhood, even after the number of nonwhite neighbors was greater than white neighbors. But over a quarter of respondents said they would try to move if the neighborhood became a third black, and over 40 percent said they would move if blacks became the majority."[1]

The data and the anecdotes combined to create a funnel that brought America to its current, inescapable place: black parents were not sadists or even experimentalists but they knew proximity to whiteness gave their children a greater chance for material success in America, and so, too, did distance from blackness. They knew it in Boston and in Milwaukee, and in all the other places where the presence of their children ignited the white anger. The farther away from blackness, the less their children might be subject to the running, the dilapidated infrastructure, the schoolbooks with the missing pages, the acceptance of substandard services just for being black. Integration was the answer but integration was a myth. In practice, integration was, ironically, the statistical embodiment of Du Bois's Talented Tenth, where, for the sake of their education, generations of black kids were, by their parents, for *their own good*, thrown against Zora Neale Hurston's proverbial white background. A hostile white background. Perhaps there would be a sprinkling of other blacks but never enough to threaten the identity of the fragile white majority that made it clear that one or two families in town would be tolerated but 30 or 40 percent—actual integration, in other words—would not.

And for their good fortune, for the sake of education, these kids would become that first generation of shape-shifters, of code-switchers, of Oreos, the only black kids in their class, who would return to their black communities untrusted and dismissed and ultimately unwelcome, penalized for their parents' aspirations for them, their authenticity on constant trial. Or they would care enough about their blackness to fight for it, fight their own and anyone else who tried to take it from them— and sometimes *still be unwelcome*. Or they would leave the black community altogether, embittered by what would feel like indirect banishment—a disinviting to the cookout—and live among whites, eternally untrusted and dismissed but also tolerated, as long as they didn't question the social order, bring any more like them to town, or ask whites to move even in the slightest toward understanding their black world. They would become a lost tribe.

I was a veteran of both camps. My parents pulled my sister and me out of the Boston public school system while we still lived in the city, extracting us from the violence of busing and enrolled us in the Metropolitan Council for Educational Opportunity, or METCO, a small, experimental program founded in 1966 in which white, suburban public schools voluntarily accepted a limited number of inner-city students whose parents would volunteer to send them. It was, ostensibly, a better option than attending inferior local schools or being subjected to the intracity busing that exposed Boston's white rage. My sister attended school in Newton, I in Waban, a third-grader and a first-grader bused an hour from home. According to this gambit, the black kids would have to wake up at 5 a.m. to go to elementary school and risk isolation in an all-white environment—and recognize the depths of their disadvantage when they saw the expanse of green space and majestic houses and backyard swings of their friends, as opposed to running across vacant lots to escape bullies. But it would all be worth it: this incarnation of the Tenth would have access to better education, better colleges, a better chance for a better life, a chance to be better than their parents, to be *better*—if they survived. And if they did, what would that survival do to them? Immersed in the white world, what would they become?

In 1977 we left Boston and moved fifty miles south to Plymouth, to "America's Hometown," the home of Plymouth Rock, the *Mayflower*, the Bradfords, the Aldens, and the supposedly benevolent Wampanoag (and later the indomitable Metacomet, but he wasn't taught in the schools; you had to wait for college and read Howard Zinn for that), and the running stopped. So, too, did the fear of the escalating dangers that one day might be too great to overcome, that would overcome my defenses because deep down I knew I wasn't really that tough. In Plymouth, at least physically, we were safe.

The threat of physical harm, however, was replaced by a different form of violence. For the continued promise of education and safety, we were separated from the black community not only during school hours, as with METCO, but permanently. METCO was replaced by being a minority full time, in school and in the neighborhood, and the potential for physical violence traded for the guarantee of the emotional: sitting in seventh-grade history class watching *Roots* while your white classmates pretended to be the slave masters and tried you by calling you

"Toby." In Plymouth, white classmates codified their belief of black illegitimacy in their language. Boom boxes were *ghetto blasters*. R&B or funk was *jungle music*. It was hearing the common response of "What am I, black?" when asking a white classmate to hand you a piece of paper, for instance, or some other menial task. It was playing street hockey with friends one day and one of their parents asking me if I was the puck. It was remembering an easygoing, biracial kid named Shawn Raymond, who sat day after day and absorbed white kids touching his hair and sticking pencils in his Afro; remembering that playing soccer in the yard of a friend's house with other kids (including Missy Gregory, a daughter of the legendary black activist Dick Gregory, who was there that day) and hearing that friend's mother, as she watched us play, say to another adult, "I don't mind her being friends with them but she better never, *ever* bring one of them home." It was recalling white friends, who *really, really liked you*, saying, "I don't mind black people, but I hate niggers."

We had walked directly into hostility. The South Shore, the fifty miles from Boston to Plymouth, had been the intended safe haven, the white-flight destination for the predominately Irish who left the city to escape busing, to escape integration, to escape black people. The whole stretch and its towns—Hingham, Marshfield, Hanover, Kingston, and Plymouth—was nicknamed the "Irish Riviera"—and, inescapably, here they were, in their paradise having to deal yet again with black people. We had fled Boston to get away from corrosive economic conditions. They had left to get away from us.

The smattering of black and Cape Verdean kids eyed one another warily, the Cape Verdeans—Silva and Fernandes, Andrade and Gomes, Barbosa and Lopes—were lighter-skinned and thus did not identify as readily as *black* and thus believed themselves to be superior in the racial hierarchy to black people. The ones who stuck together usually did so through class, as so many of the blacks and browns lived in public housing. The ones who didn't, like me, whose parents owned their homes, periodically had to take some hazing from some of the other black and browns—but that was only when they were around the white kids. I knew what they were doing: they were proving they could be just as cruel to black students as their white class-mates were. It was, in a sense, a litmus test for them to prove their loyalty to the majority-white surroundings, to prove to the other white students that under the right circumstances we were just niggers, too, even to other niggers. They, too, stood against the hostile white backdrop. They were surviving.

Implicit in this bargain, of course, was that no aspects of whiteness would be challenged. Given the numbers, so many outcomes would be predetermined: the one black boy in class would invariably be paired with the only black girl, whether or not they had anything else in common. If they didn't, the black boys would date the white girls or date no one at all, but it wasn't as easily reciprocal for the black girls because the white boys didn't want to be seen with black girls. One summer, a good friend of mine was being pursued by a Cape Verdean girl. He asked me what to do. I told him to go out with her. "But," he said quizzically (and quite certainly to the chagrin of all Cape Verdeans who thought they were special), "she's black." White-ness as culture was smothering, alleviated only by the oasis of individual relationships with white people, lifelong friends who saved my life. We outcasts discovered one another. Those whites, too, then, as those before them, and most likely those in the postracial now, paid dearly for their friendships. The white girls, treated mercilessly by the white boys they would not date—but would marry later—were nigger lovers, called so to their faces. Any of the white kids who enjoyed Prince, Michael Jackson, Run-DMC, or LL Cool J a bit too much would be accused of listening to "jungle music." (*Wigger*, another derogatory term for the white boys who liked rap or basketball and emulated black culture, came later.) Each step in this dance might have brought this lost tribe of black students closer to the *legitimate* world, closer to assimilation, to mastering a smooth navigation of the white universe that would later become their life, but it also, step by step, came at a tremendous—and for the kids unequipped for this daily warfare, traumatic—cost. It distanced these aspirational black people (at least the ones who believed in this pathway's potential) from the nurturing power of a black community, to the point where the foreign, hostile environment was no longer being the only black kid in class in a white world but being black around other black people. The iceberg had again broken off and once more black people were adrift. Outside of individual relationships with white friends, whose bonds were being tested daily both in a local and national sense, black people had no home.

Soon enough the rest of the dominoes fell: cut off from black America but always reminded they were not white, the lost tribe began to believe as white people did, believe in the myth of being self-made. They did not need a collective, historical identity because they knew they no longer had one: never white, but culturally perhaps not black. Identifying as black would always require careful negotiation instead of a simple, unequivocal "yes." They were less inclined to feel any oneness with the black and brown people around the world or to acknowledge the systemic racism that created their situation, even while often living in the public housing of a predominately white community. Some would believe in the white standards of beauty, forgive whiteness and its crushing racism while resenting the black community for what they saw as its rejection of them, the incessant battering for *talking white* or *sounding white*. Of course, white standards of beauty invaded black communities just as destructively, with black people ripping each other apart in their insults of one another for being too light or too dark. Black people using the word *black* as an insult has always been the most cutting because of its ruthless simplicity. It need not be complicated. You were the despised, even to each other. All it took was that one word to stamp you as ugly.

In college, at school gatherings and parties, the more in-secure members of the lost tribe were obvious, uncomfortable engaging even in majority-black conversational circles, the black boys wary of the other black boys, perhaps fearful of losing their exoticism with the white girls. Perhaps they weren't so special after all. These black boys had not been integrated. They had been assimilated.

The Swahili word for "lost" is *potea*, and for the second time these black people again were to be lost, except that this deal of moving fifty miles away from black roots or going to school ninety minutes from home was ostensibly voluntary, all in the name of education, all in the name of proximity to the safer, better world of whiteness. It would not be long before the black people of the lost tribe would commit what James Baldwin would call the ultimate sin of racism: hearing what white people said about them and *believing* it, believing that being black was the worst thing in the world. Against the white backdrop, no one was spared. Through middle and high school there was a bi-racial Asian classmate of mine named Matthew Gortz, a wonderfully talented athlete, especially in soccer. Once, during a break in a pickup basketball game, I grew weary and relayed some long-forgotten upsetting racial exchange, and he responded unforgettably: "What about me? I look like a fucking chink."

THE PRICE OF THE TICKET

This was the bargain. On the East Coast and West, in the Midwest. This was black people at their aspirational best, determined to leave the *dead or in jail* narratives, the redlined neighborhoods, to the ballplayers and rappers, leaving the rest of black people and the black problems behind. They could act like they made it. They were the new Tenth but also the lost tribe. What, it must be asked, was the purpose of exposing ourselves and our children to so much violence? Was it simply the promise of education, and if so, was it worth it? Or was something loftier, dreamier, even more aspirational and far more dangerous at play? Access to education is one matter. Gaining respect and love, to be seen as an equal—especially by one's historical oppressor, whose power is rooted in your suppression—is quite different. The American bargain assumes the black, the Chinese, and the Pakistani and Middle Easterner have the opportunity not just to go to Harvard and purchase a Mercedes but to do so with the respect of and in harmony with the very people who once barred them from reading or entering the country or playing Major League Baseball. There is a reckless arrogance to this sentiment, even a pathetic yearning, embraced by Americans of all races, a desire to enwrap an experiment of violence and greed and blood in a fairy-tale, Hollywood screenplay. It was not the only pathway, and indeed the fairy tale has been rejected in several instances, most obviously by many wealthy Mandarin Chinese who arrived in postwar San Francisco. After anti-Chinese real estate covenants were abolished in the late 1940s they purchased real estate beyond Chinatown, in the Richmond and Sunset districts, but did not overly assimilate on a promise of a rainbow before the final credits—they took the tangible benefits of what America offered and flushed the gauzy rest. No friendship, no dream, no mountaintop. Just equity, land, some political power—and some peace in the power of being left alone. They were often ridiculed for not assimilating. Some lived in San Francisco for fifty years and never learned English but they owned what they had and could not be moved. They didn't need to be friends.

The black story is different. There was no homeland the wealthy fled and no new country to where they brought their money, as was the case with the postrevolutionary Cubans and Mandarins. Black people, with no capital and facing enormous systemic legislative and local restrictions, required a promise that their white countrymen could overcome their common belief that blacks lacked the industriousness to succeed. There is no shortage of irony in calling the enslaved, who worked without wage from dawn to dusk, received no Homestead Act and no

GI Bill, lazy. When black aspiration did flourish, as separate as the fingers, white marauders burned its successes, its Black Wall Streets and Rosewoods, to the ground. The black story required cooperation, and no small degree of submission, for the next generation of black youth to actually be, in Maya Angelou's words, the dream of the slave. There is a mutual romance to it all, the immoral country and its enslaved chattel rehabilitated together by books and brain, opportunity and reform. It is a fantasy.

THE NEAREST SCHOOL IS JUST A FEW BLOCKS AWAY.

In 2016 METCO celebrated its fiftieth anniversary. Newspaper stories, radio interviews, and documentaries from the *Boston Globe* to NPR recalled those first generations of integrationist kids. An article about the METCO program in Concord, that famous Revolutionary War town, began with, "It's working. And no one is interested in changing a thing." Another, with the headline "For 50 Years, This Voluntary Busing Program Has Desegregated Schools 1 Family—and 1 District—at a Time," chronicled a family getting their young child up at 5 a.m. to go to school, as I did forty-five years earlier. It contained a paragraph that read:

> The Dillons live in a three-story, early 20th century home in the historic, largely working-class, predominantly black neighborhood of Dorchester in south Boston. His father owns an auto repair shop, and his mother is a grant specialist; both grew up in the neighborhood. The nearest public school is just a few blocks away. But every morning, the Dillons put Collin on a bus that takes him 90 minutes or more out of the city to a public elementary school in the coastal community of Marblehead.

The stories were hopeful. They were frustrating. They invoked the violent roots of the 1960s and 1970s—the riots, the white attacks on black kids trying to attend white schools—that cried out for interracial solutions, the genesis of METCO's birth. They were personal, now that so many of the former METCO children were adults. They existed at a time of national reconsideration, especially among black families faced with another generation of the same bargain. Among the emotional shrapnel, they had begun a reassessment of the idea that proximity to whiteness is best for black children, unsure a better way existed. The *New York Times* wrote about the difficulties of black students at the predominately white Ivy League schools. The *Atlantic* offered a long profile about the perils of minority students at elite private schools.

For all the triumph, an obvious question was not asked: why, after a half century, is METCO still necessary? Fifty years later the black kids in their black communities are still running from the violence, their parents still getting them up at 5 a.m., still with a school nobody wants to go to just a few blocks away, often still underserving the community. As the retrospectives piled up in Boston, the outrage that fifty years later many black parents still believe the best educational opportunity for their six-year-olds is to put them on a bus for a daily three-hour round-trip commute to school—reinforcing the belief that becoming a member of the lost tribe is a necessity—was largely and curiously nonexistent. Less discussed were the structural impediments to black educational opportunity. In 2019 the educational nonprofit EdBuild estimated that predominately white school districts received $23 billion more in educational funding than schools in predominately black districts. In celebrating its anniversary, METCO reported that ten thousand children were on its waiting list.

The Supreme Court did ask the question, and in 2007 concluded that METCO and programs like it around the country *weren't* necessary; not because America's cities had dedicated themselves to improving the local school systems with the type of concerted public works efforts required to create vibrant black communities with education at their center, but because, as the conservative court determined in *Community Schools v. Seattle School District No. 1*, public school systems are forbidden to consider the racial identity of students as a method of promoting integration. Black parents were not entitled to satisfactory local schools and the country's highest court had determined they were not going to be aided in being aspirational, either. The decision was another example of the post–*Brown vs. Board of Education* opposition machine in action, an adjunct to the 1974 *Milliken* decision that excluded suburban public school districts from participating in efforts to desegregate schools, and a forgotten foundation of Ronald Reagan's political career was a hostility toward desegregation and an aggression toward its destruction. Even the argument that cities have begun investing in public schools, making programs like METCO less relevant, does so relying on the sleight of hand of public charter schools, which siphon money away from existing public systems under the guise of "school choice." These post-*Brown* educational covenants all have the same effect of keeping local schools segregated and inferior, which explains why, a half century later, METCO is still necessary. Where there are black communities, there is corruption on the part of the state and private industry to deprive those communities of their potential services and vibrancy. When the black community is vibrant or the land valuable, redevelopment is inevitable. New York City currently offers property tax abatements to spur gentrification. Integration is the only solution and yet the remedies, available to the select few aspirational black families with the resources to take this risk, are always on white terms.

The lost tribe was created not only by aspirational black parents but by the American legal machinery. Full-scale desegregation was prohibited by courts and local schools remained inferior, leaving those black parents with ambition, means, and vision essentially two choices: find one of the handful of predominately black school districts in the country that are thriving or throw their children against the hostile white background. We either lose opportunity or lose ourselves.

It is a reconsideration that has vindicated my Aunt Judy, who during the days of desegregation in Boston never underestimated the emotional violence that came with pulling her kids away from the black community. She attended Jeremiah E. Burke High School in Dorchester with my mother. My mother decided to place her children into the proximity of whiteness. My aunt, her best friend, rejected the upward potential of the lost tribe. The cost was just too high.

"I understood the conversations that were taking place and I knew that the kids were not necessarily getting the education that we received when I was in school," she told me when I asked her why she and my uncle didn't move my cousins out of Boston during busing, as my parents had moved us. "But if there were things they weren't learning, we felt we could teach them at home. But you couldn't just rinse away the effects of that kind of isolation. We didn't want to expose our children to it. You might have access to nicer things but you could lose your sense of self, your identity. And if you did, you might not ever regain it."

THE WORST THING IN THE WORLD

I have said, to the point of nausea, that only two acceptable avenues exist for discussing race in the United States: acknowledge *things are better than they were* or *get over it.* Neither of these options has ever served black people, the actual primary targets of American racism. Neither sentiment addresses what it means to be part of a lost tribe, to be the only nigger in class, to know that by this vulgarity is how your classmates view you, simultaneously considering your presence to be proof of progress and you to be a friend. Certainly, neither makes an ally of the speaker, and this is true even when—or especially when—the speaker of *get over it* is black. Both demand that black people appreciate how good they have it. If it feels threatening, it most certainly is, for the tone betrays the true goal: the welcome arrival of the day when black people will finally stop talking about race, which will also mean the arrival of the day when white people can stop listening to it. From that day forward America will no longer need to reflect upon its unexamined, devastating history, nothing will need to change, and we can all get on with it. The goal of discussing race in this country is not to illuminate a society but to silence a people.

But what is *it*, exactly, that we're getting on with? *It* means making a reality of commonplace racial clichés about a "colorblind" society, where America's racial chasms will be solved by people who don't "see" color. What they mean, of course, isn't to not see color but to specifically not see black, not hear black, not have to deal with black. "For the generality of white Americans," James Baldwin said in 1984, "the word 'progress' really involves how quickly and how thoroughly a black person becomes white. That's all it really means."

In a kind world, the notion of colorblindness might be viewed as inspirational. In America, which is not kind and has reams of evidence to prove it, Baldwin's view makes manifest a ruthless assault on the black identity masquerading as progress that is not futuristic or theoretical but is happening, actively, and with devastating results. It does not begin with the ostensibly disposable lower classes, upon whom in the dystopian visions of science-fiction literature social experimentations take place, but with the black aristocracy, the Ones Who Made It, with the heirs of Du Bois's Talented Tenth. That a black person become thoroughly white is the great unspoken demand that is not a grim forecast, hysteria, but a foundational prerequisite. It is the through line that exists across all occupations in post–Jim Crow America but is practiced most overtly in sports, where the most successful black employees this country has ever produced spend their time not leveraging their hard-worn success to advocate for a greater share of the American dream, but minimizing their own identity, being less assertive in the one industry where they possess the most power. The athlete is at the forefront of a certain type of trade: assimilation in exchange for money and star status affixed with serious conditions. The manifestations of such barter are especially chilling, for if blackness cannot be expressed where black people are dominant culturally and financially, what possible hope is there for African Americans in the fields in which they are not?

"I'M NOT BLACK. I'M O.J."—O. J. SIMPSON, 1969

Who among us would not want to be considered self-created? To be seen as such is to be free of historical constraint and therefore moral liability—as well as responsibility. It is the great

American seduction. There would be no past and no heirs, no benefactors and no circumstances. And there would be no debt. It would embody that most coveted of American archetypes— "self-made." *A self-made man.* A self-made millionaire, even better. A self-made billionaire, better still. The freedom would be limitless, for if one can truly become self-made, then we all can. There are then no limitations, no castes, no systems, no shackles from birth. The only constraints are the one the individual places upon oneself.

It is an illusion and the adolescence embedded within this racial libertarianism is obvious. Many an Old West myth-turned-popular culture–turned-history has been based upon it, conveniently omitting the government assistance for white people of policies like the Homestead Act, political aggression backed by the muscle of the US Army. Yet, the allure of the myth is all-encompassing. It is the anchor of modern American conservatism. Rugged individualism is the American credo. Clarence Thomas, benefactor of affirmative action, the closest policy his country has ever come to acknowledging its systemic crimes against his people, supposedly keeps his Yale law degree in the basement of his house because of its apparent taint. He does this though it is implausible to assume he would have become a Supreme Court justice without it. Thomas said in his 2007 memoir that he appraised his Ivy League law degree at fifteen cents because affirmative action undermined his degree from earned to given.* Thomas had been trained well. Instead of holding his country accountable for all it had not done for hundreds of thousands of preceding Clarence Thomases—many presumably much smarter than he—Thomas, while being proud of what he had done with his individual opportunity, dutifully chose the myth of being self-made. He rejected his own hard work as a handout.

---

* Thomas always could have elected to refuse his Supreme Court nomination if he truly believed his pathway was illegitimate. He chose not to take such a drastic, morally consistent step.

O. J. Simpson, America's first crossover superstar black athlete, craved the self-made myth and created an enduring template. Positioning himself as a wholly original entity with no ancestry, Simpson calculated, would be the key to the Good Life: access to the cars the whites owned without being an assumed member of the underworld, to the big houses in the good neighborhoods inhabited only by whites, to the Hollywood white women whom the culture anointed the pinnacle of beauty, unattainable to him, the exclusive golf club memberships whose bylaws excluded him. If only he could become self-made and not black, entrée into respectability awaited. What followed was the birth of a credo: *I'm not black. I'm O.J.*

Being O.J. and not black freed him from the worst thing in the world, which was to be black in a society that despises black people and punishes blackness. He decided his sinews had created something out of nothing and he would go as far as his abilities carried him. He was now self-made.

The illusion of being self-made allowed the despised to believe they were ridding themselves of their caste and reinventing themselves on their own terms—and even, if they were willing to entertain the dark corners of the mind, to use their presence to infiltrate, to exact revenge on the world for calling them despised in the first place. Instead, O.J. was purchased. The money changed hands and the commercials followed. Hertz. Dingo. Spot-Bilt. The movies were next. The legacy formed and future players followed the bread crumbs O.J. had left for them. The money got bigger and the voices got smaller, even as the issues remained urgent. The strategy served the white bosses who ran professional sports even better than it did him, for Simpson—and not Curt Flood, Tommie Smith, or John Carlos, who believed their prominence increased their duty to improve conditions for black people—had laid the foundation for how black athletes should behave. When it was Michael Jordan's turn, he followed the trail, codifying the template.

By that point, Jim Brown had already endorsed Nixon *and*

Reagan and it was the talented, black despised, let in on the action because a handful of them could run and dunk, who best held up their end of the bargain: silent, apolitical, detached, and rich beyond belief while many of the social conditions of their childhoods worsened. Meanwhile, instead of being grateful for not being despised, white men and women ratcheted their anger and sneered with self-made defiance ("nobody handed me anything"). The more affluent and accomplished the white person, the more tightly he or she clung to being self-made. Howard Schultz, the Starbucks coffee magnate, benefactor of the public school system, where taxes paid for his education, exemplified this attitude as he considered a presidential bid in 2019. It was a defense mechanism against the blunt force of the truth: their whiteness led to a pipeline of connections that led to handshakes that led to a résumé that would find its way to just the right desk. No one may have handed them anything but neither was a system of legal and extralegal racial barriers actively working against them.

The myth, however, is a critical component of white identity: if whites don't recognize a structure reinforced by violence aiding them, there conversely can be no labyrinth of barriers or violence impeding anyone else. By this logic there is no structure at all, for or against, and therefore nothing and no one for those blacks to blame and no system that whites owe as their benefactor. A 2016 criminal justice survey by the Cato Institute reported 40 percent of whites believed the criminal justice system treated whites more fairly, compared with 72 percent of African Americans who believed criminal justice favored whites. White individual success is allowed to be self-made as surely as black failure is its own, and the political silence of the black successful—"What racism? Look at M.J.!"—can be employed to amplify this erroneousness. America can be seen as a heroic, egalitarian experiment created not from murder and subjugation but diligence and hard work.

I am reminded of a long-ago conversation I had in college

with Gerry Foeman, my sociology professor at Temple University, whose mind was brilliant. He was the first black male instructor (who wasn't a gym teacher) of my life. I once approached him for advice on coalition building and expressed frustration with the lack of interest that students of other minority groups, most specifically Asian students, had in joining African Americans in what at the time seemed to me to be a common struggle.

"They've already been programmed, especially the foreign students, to stay away from you," he explained. "They know to stay away from you before they even get here. Think about how the world sees you: you're the violent, the pimp, the rapist, the pusher. You're the criminals bringing society down, holding it back. This is your cultural export. It's what the world thinks about you. It makes perfect sense they don't want anything to do with you. Who would want to be associated with a loser?"

To be O.J. and not black meant being unstuck from the pathologies that occur worldwide but stick to black people. It meant not being a loser. It meant the seductions of the American Dream could also belong to him and a pathway out of the constraints of blackness suddenly appeared, like a gap between the tackles, an opening produced by money and celebrity. For both the despisers and the despised, money could make the transition possible, unsticking the black ones lucky enough to have world-class speed, a buttery singing voice, or a brain that could get them into Harvard, allowing them to move to the good life and away from the worst thing in the world. All they had to do was run toward it and leave the rest behind.

Of course, being unstuck *is* a myth. The ones that weren't so lucky, the ones whose singing voice wasn't so buttery, well, the self-made could dismiss them by suggesting they just weren't determined enough. But the fantasy collapses when the talented ones find themselves in unfamiliar territory, confronted, for instance, by the pedestrian white authority figure who doesn't recognize the black man standing in his driveway isn't some ghetto kid shoveling snow to make money in a rich neighborhood but is Doug Glanville, former Major League Baseball player and Princeton grad; or when the New Jersey state police didn't realize the black man they racially profiled in his $150,000 Bentley was not a Newark drug kingpin but John Saunders, the late ESPN broadcaster. In these environments, or in O.J.'s, when his life collapsed and suddenly his legal team needed his blackness to again matter, money-created insulations could not save them. They were no longer self-made. They were suddenly stuck after all.

"I'M NOT BLACK. I'M CABLINASIAN"—TIGER WOODS, 2000

One of the key recommendations of the landmark 1968 Kerner Commission report that followed the riots of the 1960s was the hiring of more black reporters to more accurately cover the needs and concerns of black communities. Who tells the story is just as important, and sometimes more important, than the story itself. Over the next quarter century, more black journalists entered the mainstream media than in all of America's previous history, ostensibly to incorporate the isolated black community—isolated both geographically and socially—into the multicultural mainstream. During the 1970s and 1980s the foundation of modern black journalism was being laid with the expectation that a pioneering wave of reporters would give voice to the voiceless. William Raspberry, Claude Lewis, Chuck Stone, Acel Moore, Bob Maynard, Brenda Payton, Claire Smith, and so many more. Even the government in those times believed that for the country to survive, blackness needed to be part of the national discourse. Yet when the first generation passed the baton, a large number of the next chose a different course: it, too, decided, like O.J., that it wanted racial libertarianism. It wanted to be self-made.

The lament was echoed and parried by black professionals across the country: "I don't want to be a *black* writer. I just want to be a writer" stood next to its twin: "I'm not a *black* doctor. I'm just a doctor who *happens* to be black." The reflex, of course, was one of navigation, a reaction to being battered by a generation of Reaganism, to the hostilities and pigeonholing of a white world that felt no hesitation to say to a black person's face that affirmative action is the only reason you have a job, the pressures and demands of the black, and the human, desire for individuality, the need to strike one's own course. Nevertheless, I cannot recall a single white writer—even among those who earn a living writing primarily about black subjects or issues—lamenting or diluting their whiteness. The navigation reached the same destination: being black was ballast to be shed, and if it could not be shed, it needed to be neutralized.

Tiger Woods did not invent erasure but he would become one of its most prominent, important, and tragic practitioners. If O.J. felt no social responsibility to the economic and political status of black people, he nevertheless understood the currency that came with being black. Being black made him an American success story, the self-made superstar in the white world. It made him unique. It made him an aspiration. It made him money, increased his commercial and sex appeal. Woods took the extraordinary step of erasing the idea of being black itself. O.J. erased blackness as a political anchor. Tiger did both, first adopting an apolitical posture then reducing his black heritage altogether by referring to himself as "Cablinasian," a composite created during his adolescence to describe what he referred to as his Caucasian, black, and Asian heritage. In the one industry where black people dominated the nationwide imagination, the culture and the talent, its superstars actively practiced erasure, avoiding comment on even the most pedestrian of current events, often growing annoyed at even the remotest suggestions of advocating for a black concern.

Many resisted but every black professional in America understood the impulse. Abandoning black people politically meant an easier life. It meant more money, a vacation house on Martha's Vineyard or maybe Nantucket or in the Hamptons. It meant a greater possibility of job security. It meant an email inbox that did not include as much vitriol from white readers and but did include platitudes from those same readers for being reasonable, which is to say accommodating to whites. Abandoning black advocacy first made the white mainstream more comfortable, as nothing would be asked of them, and it transformed the black professional into someone who might be enlisted in calming the black community. Mostly, it provided so many white bosses with what they truly sought, which was diversity of color (to keep *their* bosses happy) without diversity of thought.

It also meant being left alone, free of the news cycle whenever something occurred to black people, because now *they* were not *you*. Dwayne Johnson and Maya Rudolph, black people who have earned millions in part by profiting off of their racial ambiguity, know this. Besides, separating from the black world was what you were *supposed* to do: black people know this well, and if whites chose to reflect, they would hear it in their own speech, the number of instances when famous black people aren't really "black" anymore or their white admirers no longer see them as "black." The American narrative demands that black people of any promise separate themselves from the lot of the despised, leave them behind. The black athlete is urged to leave his surroundings and never return. He found his "way out." They will hear they are no longer "black" but have *transcended race*.

There was a day, probably one of those moments staring out of an airplane window heading to this World Series, that Wimbledon, or countless games in between, when I had a thought: success in America routinely correlated to the distance from black people. The farther away, the brighter the prospects. The schools were better. The food was healthier. The streets were safer. The services were more plentiful, the real estate more desirable. Even the greatest black commodity—its athletes— eventually rejected black colleges for the established white universities that for decades never wanted them. The same was true when the topic was black advocacy: the greater the political commitment to the black community, the greater the professional jeopardy. It explained why even discussing current events seemed such a wrenching struggle for so many prominent black professionals, particularly the visible players who seemed to have so much control. They composed large majorities in basketball and football, both at the big-time college and professional levels, yet knew that being identified with African Americans—unless there were millions to be made off of the cool factor of black culture—was a liability. Who, after all—as Dr. Foeman asked me that day years ago—wants to be associated with a loser?

What does one do when the ballast cannot be tossed over, when the money and the material do not provide the promised protection? What does one do with the realization that, even with money, one cannot ever be completely unstuck, as Tiger discovered when his 2017 DUI arrest sheet classified his race as "black"? What often follows is a suffocating self-hatred, a wrestle with which came first: despising oneself or being despised so deeply by one's country that inevitably one starts to believe it. The alternative to self-hatred, of course, is love, and more specifically a deep and permanent self-love that provides a more durable, impenetrable protection than a BMW or closing on a house in a predominately white neighborhood ever could. It provides for black people a home, a refuge, an inheritance, *a heritage*. Accepting that love, believing in its nurturing qualities, requires imagination and courage and a firmness of conviction that being black is *not* the worst thing in the world, or even a liability— except when being assessed through the lens of whiteness.

Instead of the grounding kind of love, black professionals often amputate, for their love of self is immediately repositioned as a threat. Less discussed is why their amputation is such an American imperative—and to whom. Just what was so horribly wrong with being a black writer in the same way Hemmingway reveled in his virility, McCourt in his elegiac Irishness, Solnit in her uncompromising feminism? When writers and other black professionals distance themselves from black advocacy as a prerequisite or inevitability of their success, they have chosen amputation. The message to every black child who wants to become them is that they are wrong to aspire to proudly claim the black voice, to take the people with them. Tiger was willing to amputate, saying in effect: I have a Stanford education. I have nearly a billion dollars in wealth. I'm the greatest in the world at what I do. I can be anything I want . . . but I'm not *that*.

"I'M JUST ME. I'M MADISON."—MADISON KEYS, 2015

In what other way was any of this to end? Professional athletes are only the most visible examples, but what is being asked of them—demanded, really—is the same demand for erasure being made of black people in virtually all corners of America. What they are being told is not that America isn't racist but that the players must be comfortable accepting it. Otherwise, challenging police or gerrymandering or the obvious hiring imbalances or other important issues from a position of black advocacy would not be accompanied by such dire consequences. But black athletes who do take public, antiracist political positions can expect the full weight of their industry—owners, coaches, media, fans, and most teammates—to punish them. They would become outcasts, active enemies within their industries, weakening their job prospects and endorsement opportunities, increasing the daily stress in jobs that are competitive and difficult enough as it is. They become *problems*. Or they will be ignored by the industry friends and teammates they thought they had. All of this is the human cost of supporting blackness even in the heavily integrated industry of professional sports, the industry that was supposed to prove the existence of the American meritocracy. These outcomes are not theoretical but make up a fifty-year roll call of casualties.

The punishment is severe and even the president was not spared. Barack Obama specifically supported black people and felt the wrath of whiteness: first, after admonishing a Cambridge,

Massachusetts, police officer for arresting the Harvard professor Henry Louis Gates Jr. for breaking into his own home after locking himself out; and second, after expressing support for the family of Trayvon Martin.

After the Gates incident, Obama even sat down for a "beer summit" with the arresting officer, a rank-and-file cop who should have been disciplined for not using basic common sense. But the black president of the United States, the most powerful man in the world, felt compelled to answer to an average local cop from an average local police department. On another occasion, Obama fired former Agriculture Department official Shirley Sherrod when the right-wing *Breitbart News* edited a speech she gave in a way that distorted her meaning and portrayed her as a racist. Obama and his administration caved in to it out of fear of right-wing criticism. Sherrod settled her defamation suit against *Breitbart* after an embarrassed Obama administration offered her another job, which she refused, but the highest office in the land was checked when occupied by a black person.

Sports will pay its field hands handsomely—just ask the black members of the Dallas Cowboys—in exchange for amputation but it will not tolerate black advocacy. Whether adopting an O.J.-birthed rejection of blackness or the Tiger Woods sleight-of-hand identity game, a template followed by Yankees stars Aaron Judge and Derek Jeter, it is understood that amputation is the cost of those millions.

The through line continued to Madison Keys in tennis, who responded to being America's African American heir to Venus and Serena Williams in a July 4, 2016, profile on the ESPN website The Undefeated with the headline "The Next Great Black Tennis Star Isn't Black or White. It's Madison Keys." The piece, written by ESPN's LZ Granderson, begins:

> Madison Keys' favorite movie is *Pretty Woman*. Her favorite actress is Julia Roberts. If a movie is ever made about her life, she wants Roberts to play her. . . . Madison

Keys is black—at least according to us. . . . In a 2015 *New York Times* profile, Keys said, "I don't really identify myself as white or African-American. I'm just me. I'm Madison."

The year following Granderson's profile, at the US Open, where Arthur Ashe had won the tournament's first men's title in 1968, where eleven years earlier Althea Gibson had won the US Nationals, the forerunner to the US Open, where Venus Williams and Serena Williams had spawned a generation of African American tennis-playing girls, Madison Keys and black tennis player Sloane Stephens met in the women's final. They are the only pair of black women to meet in a grand slam final other than Venus and Serena, the greatest siblings professional sports has ever produced.

Leading up to the final weekend, which in the country club sport of tennis featured three African Americans—Keys, Stephens, and Venus—in the four semifinal slots, the excitement of the moment engulfed the grounds. American women's tennis, long lagging outside the enormous shadow of Venus and Serena, was back. Black American tennis, played in the largest tennis stadium in the world, named after Ashe, the sport's most inspirational player, was featured. The lineage dating back to Gibson—who became the first African American, male or female, to win a major championship in 1956 when she won the French Championships—was obvious to the multitude of fans, especially the young black girls who were now inspired to play tennis by them, just as a young Madison Keys had been inspired to play tennis from watching Venus Williams. Everyone, from black United States Tennis Association president and CEO Katrina Adams to black USTA director of player development Martin Blackman, was inspired by the continuation of the black heritage in tennis. Everyone, that is, except Madison Keys, who during a national moment of black pride—she of the African American father, inspired to play the game by the legendary

Venus Williams and herself inspiring young black girls—reiterated that weekend that she was essentially neutral. She did not identify as black or white and saw herself being played in a biopic by Julia Roberts.

No past. No heirs. No benefactors and—no debt.

There is, however, nothing neutral about Madison Keys. This is true because there is nothing neutral about the American racial order. None of this, it should be noted, is to suggest Madison Keys is obligated to embrace her blackness, be political, or live any life that is inauthentic for Madison Keys. However she carries herself is a choice that is personal to her, and regardless of her status as a public figure, a private one.

What it does demand, however, is an acknowledgment that a choice *is* being made, and that choice is a conscious one. By saying she chooses neither racial identification, Keys is choosing the default, which is the majority, and that is whiteness. It can be seen through the obviousness of her choices, the porous racial libertarianism that accompanies them. Blackness is the one racial identity that comes with both responsibility and cost, and whether as a defense mechanism, fear of controversy, or authentic disconnection to black America, the choice for someone with a black parent to publicly and repeatedly proclaim no identification as African American is a deliberate one. The reflex to communicate to black people, "Do not count on me. Do not count on me at all. Do not ask me for anything," is not one that comes by happenstance but is a surrender to all the forces imploring one to avoid the devastating consequences that will follow. If the beach is covered with signs, each more perilous than the last—"Rip Tide," "Shark Warning," "Toxic Waste"—who would leap in and take a swim?

Retreat from black identity is the by-product of many forces, and when it comes to muting the black voice, there are so many forces at work. Athletes' careers depend on a certain conformity. The strategic choice of not speaking about civil rights is often a tactical exercise in survival, but it is also yet another example of surrendering to overwhelming odds, odds that have deep roots. There are few spaces where challenging racial norms is encouraged, never mind accepted, and given the template for class elevation for black families over the past half century—which has generally required leaving the resource-poor black communities for the resource-plentiful white ones—the black child who grows into the black professional has been discouraged for virtually all of their life from identifying with being unconditionally black. I have always been confounded by the black parents who placed their children in overwhelmingly white settings, only to grow frustrated when their kids grew more comfortable around whites, dated or married interracially, and identified more (or completely) with an integrated community rather than a traditional black experience. Even the term "an integrated community" is generous, and wholly inaccurate. As studies show that white families will invariably leave if too many black families move in, what black families are entering is not "an integrated community" but a white one. Black people are no different from anyone else; they adapt to their environment, and whether or not it is embraced personally, whiteness becomes the habitat of people who live within it, no different from urbanicity or rurality. In any other setting one becomes what one lives and doing so is uncontroversial. Yet only by the sheer fact of their blackness are African Americans expected to live in predominately white environments and still identify with the experiences, surroundings, and people of a black community they very well may not know. They are expected to do this also while absorbing the attitudinal (and sometimes physical) hostility toward blackness commonplace in the white world. There is a certain inevitability to the situation and that inevitability is the eventual erasure of a black sensibility. It is by design. It is the consequence of assimilation without actual integration and there is nothing neutral about it.

Fighting and overcoming these forces is so daunting that identifying as black becomes a political choice.

OUT OF NOWHERE

In baseball, a key to hitting is to "look fastball and adjust to the curve." The philosophy is based on the fact that a fastball has too much velocity for a batter to prepare for any other pitch, while a curve ball is just slow enough for a hitter to be able to make a split-second correction and make contact on a pitch they weren't expecting. The weapon of the curve ball is not just its deception but its unpredictability. You don't know when it's coming or exactly how to follow it.

For the 2019–20 television season, ABC greenlit *Mixed-ish*, a spinoff of its popular comedy *Black-ish*. The premise is an origin story set in 1985, centering Rainbow "Bow" Johnson, a main character on *Black-ish*, and her childhood family as they transitioned from living on a multiracial commune to mainstream suburbia. The trailer for the show is full of tropes that appear harmless. Bow and her siblings are biracialized outcasts trying to fit in but not quite belonging in any traditional racial group. They are depicted as starry-eyed former commune kids with exotic features, so sheltered by compound living that they don't even recognize an ice maker or a water gun.

Then there's the gun-loving, white conservative grandfather who hangs a picture of Ronald Reagan on the wall and reminds the family he's in charge; the hippie parents who avoid the imperatives of color in favor of love; and the forebodingly mean black kids at school (some of whom, we are to assume, will eventually come around). Everyone gets lampooned and the sharp, defining borders have their trauma-inducing points smoothed down, leaving room for all. (The trailer even shows the squeezably cute youngest running with her newfound water gun, yelling, "I love the Second Amendment!") "It's hard to be Rainbow," the trailer cleverly teases, "in a black-and-white world."

For a country desperate to delude itself into believing its fractures come from mere differences in philosophy and not white racial aggression, the inclusion of these stereotypes as quirky and benign is a sly ruse designed to assuage fears of white audiences through comic relief. For mixed-raced children, even in the dark ages of 1985, there was no such thing as a black-and-white world. If you had a black parent, there was only one world, and it was the black world. You may have been mixed, but culturally and in the eyes of the dominant white society—and more important, the law—you were black. Even more importantly, whether you lived in a white community or a predominately black one or some rare place in between, you weren't white. You may have alternately suffered and benefited from the colorism that corrodes the black community but you were still black. And if you ever thought otherwise, someone, somewhere reminded you of this fact of history, and probably harshly.

The show's trailer lists a montage of biracial celebrities and world figures today's mixed-race kids can emulate—Colin Kaepernick, Halle Berry, Barack Obama, and Meghan Markle—while failing to mention that each and every one not only personally identifies as black but is seen as such by the white world.

Where is the utility in 2020 for this redefinition? It is rooted in antiblackness, using biracialism and class as an ally of whiteness when historically children of mixed-race couples may not have seen themselves as completely black, though they were never allowed to be white. There is today a value to white society in isolating blackness, whether geographically by community or culturally by class, if one is fortunate enough financially to have the choice to be isolated, and especially politically. The whiteness of a mixed-race child was never claimed by white people but redefining the terms of race is the pinnacle of racism or its foundation, or both. The redefining is not an act of tolerance. It's an act of power. And after centuries when one drop of black blood disqualified an entire people from equality in America, with their white relatives often denying their existence, television has now decided to portray biracialism as a harmless choice between units of equal value (or its own unique category—an asset, even), when those units have been anything but equal. Now that is acceptable to be mixed and not be forced to identify as black, biracialism, too, can be enlisted to isolate blackness. Who, in other words—the words of Robert Kennedy, in fact—would willfully choose to trade places with its black citizens?

How else, then, having seen the road map and witnessed the roadkill, could black players be expected to act? To act another way, given the demands the professional sports world places on athletes to be inoffensive to the predominately white ticket buyers, would be willfully entering the dissident space. For the past half century, support for the black and the brown has been viewed as an indictment of the white—and perhaps it is—for at some point white Western society must answer for its history. The player who demands an answer places his or her entire professional career in jeopardy. More than ever, identifying as black becomes a dangerous political choice.

In 2014, Dwight Howard, then of the Houston Rockets, tweeted out a hashtag #FreePalestine, and for that high crime was castigated as an anti-Semite. He issued a painful, groveling apology, explained that he was "mistaken" and would "never" discuss international politics, and removed the tweet after fifteen minutes. Less than an hour later, one of Howard's teammates, the Israeli player Omri Casspi, unapologetically sent out a tweet denouncing Palestine. There was no outrage, no apology, and no diluted cry for "unity."

What, then, do so many of these black people—the leaders, the role models, the superstars of the celebrity class, the supposed proof that racial barriers in America are really just self-imposed—have to show for their success? They certainly do not have real power, for they know that the mere public support of a black political position threatens their employment. Nor have they received a more benign America for their acquiescence, for it responded to their success of what is possible in America by electing Donald Trump.

What the successful black person has received in this exchange, often in wild abundance, is money. Tiger Woods wasn't attempting to be accurate when he called himself Cablinasian because no one was calling him white. He wasn't reasserting his mother's Thai or his father's Native American heritage because no one ever devalued it. He called himself Cablinasian only because the world was calling him black, just as the world called Madison Keys black, and she rejected that. Accompanying the Baldwin prophecy is a cultural pressure to agree to a bargain so enormous that it resembles a rite of passage, a privilege. Or perhaps the bargain is even more sinister, not to transform the black into white but to ensure the black becomes antiblack. Black people can be claimed as success stories as long as they are willing to abandon the black people who need them politically and socially. They are well compensated and the white mainstream order remains unthreatened. Everybody wins, except those black people who look in the mirror and actually like what they see.

WHY TONYA?

How do stories get told? Who tells them, who decides which ones reach the public, and how are they framed are all questions as important as the stories themselves. The ideas and concepts that do not emerge from this winnowing process suffer a fate worse than being forgotten: to the public, they never existed. The choosing of a protagonist tells an audience where their focus will be and what values, by proximity to the protagonist, will be linked to virtue. It tells in whose success the public should make an emotional investment. Conversely, the choice of protagonist will also tell the audience in whom not to invest, for whoever is not granted these important traits and is distanced from virtue is positioned as the opposite, an antagonist, and will be seen as suspicious, shadowy, disposable.

Inside of these questions, naturally, is power, and whoever has it, with the pen, the camera, the contracts and the dollars, has a form of omnipotence. They set the landscape, the rules, and the tensions. They tell us who should receive our sympathy and who should not. They, in a way, become the creators of truth. With the country's brutal and living history looming on every page of every screenplay or manuscript, the tension in these choices is the reinterpretation of America. Who is the freedom fighter and who is the terrorist? Now that the historically voiceless can finally speak, have had the temerity to run for president (and win), and believe they, too, own a leading role in shaping the American narrative, inclusion is a primary weapon of the storytelling battlefield.

No longer can it be accepted as fact that cowboys and Indians present clear moral opposites, or that homesteading can exist without genocide, or that police are heroes and troops are liberators. Or that every leading character of every story will be white. With storytelling in different hands, these frameworks now receive direct challenge, and with power shifting hands, yesterday's heroes just might be tomorrow's murderers.

"Inclusion" may sound like a feel-good word, but it is deceivingly sharp. It is an indictment softening harder themes such as *erasure, discrimination, whitewashing*. The Pulitzer Prize–winning reporter David Maraniss once said of journalism that "history writes people out of the story and it's our job to write them back in." Inclusion is another word for this retrofitting, meaning reviving the forgotten stories, telling the Rashomon-style angles of the existing ones, challenging the story we've been told with more stories. When the camera is passed around, the story changes. Inclusion also is a kind way of detonating the American roadside explosive that is race. At some point during these conversations that turn into debates, that reveal the deep creases in the American experience, white people will invite cliché. "Well," they often conclude, "history is written by the winners." It is oft used, cynical, and an admission: history is rarely truth as much as it is propaganda for the last people standing.

There is a lesson in this for contemporary times. The last people standing are generally what we call the mainstream. They are, to follow the cliché, the winners. They want to be told the triumphant story of their victory again and again, and being the winners, they are in all the right positions to have that happen. Without competing and complementing versions of the truth, without the history that was written out, what is left is not only the original killing but the ability of the winners to kill future generations in perpetuity.

Repetition provides rehabilitation. It provides reinforcement. The same story of valor with the same people possessing the same virtue (and the same opposition displaying the same pathologies with no opportunity for redemption) becomes fact, as other storytellers may try different formulas but they repeat the narrative, with the same winners winning, and with honor. When enough generations see enough adaptations that reach the same conclusion, it becomes culture. Rehabilitation as entertainment is a successful device for many segments of white America because it is essential that white people view themselves as just plain folk made good and not treaty breakers, workers not rapists, adventurers not conquerors. Even the conquered will soon believe in the goodness of the conqueror. It is the only way to maintain the myth of American fairness, the myth of the conquerors' exceptionalism.

REHAB ASSIGNMENTS

Having lived for nearly a quarter century best known for infamously arranging the kneecapping of her greatest figure-skating rival before the 1994 Winter Olympics, a decision was made that Tonya Harding's version of the truth needed to be heard. The decision was made at Disney, where ABC News and ESPN both released Tonya Harding television retrospectives, and by Craig Gillespie, director of the 2017 Hollywood film *I, Tonya*. Her rehabilitation season had begun.

The entertainment possibilities were endless, with the upper-crust and genteel sport of figure skating being the backdrop of a hit job. The Keystone Kops wackiness of the story made Harding a "news of the weird" fixture for two and a half decades, but in Gillespie's skilled hands, the bunglers were mere comic relief. The real story was the decision to position disgraced Tonya Harding, of all people, as a representative of something poignant and bittersweet about ourselves, told in fourth-wall style, with Harding looking into the camera, talking directly to the audience. After years of ridicule she was no longer the defendant but the righteous prosecution. Her character, played by Margot Robbie, was white tears without the tears, combative, unrepentant. One review encompassed much of the response to the film, stating that the "astoundingly gifted, working-class" Harding received a "compassionate, hugely entertaining reappraisal," and adding that the film was a "totally satisfying retelling of a story we thought we knew." The film's trailer, voiced over by Robbie, rests on the power of perspective. In it, Harding represents herself while inadvertently speaking for the times, saying, "There's no such thing as truth. Everyone has their own truth."

In an indictment that the most insignificant black American could make of their country—and far more convincingly—Tonya looks directly into the camera, talking to her countrymen, and says, "You did this to me, America." She forces audiences to listen to her critique of their grotesque celebrity teardown culture. And hear her it does, without calling her a whiner for blaming society for her problems, without telling her to get over it. When Tonya's father leaves his broken marriage and walks out the door—abandoning not just his wife but also his daughter/prodigy—this dysfunctional white family dynamic doesn't stick like gum to the bottom of one's shoe, unable to be removed, as it does to the struggling black family. Her father's tires screech down the road; at one point in the scene, one wonders if young Tonya will have to leap out of the way to avoid Dad running her over with his car on his way to freedom.

He leaves and we, the audience, are expected to feel something profoundly sad for her. Perhaps we should. We black moviegoers—who have had the absent-father narrative affixed to us like a tattoo, pathologized as the irredeemable ruin of the black household, the harbinger of teen pregnancy, gangs, drugs, murder, and irresponsibility, turned into cliché by every NBA and NFL success story ("You the real MVP")—see something different. We see luxury. We see the luxury of life getting in the way of a family being a family, and instead of being viewed as a drain on society, Gillespie refines their brokenness into fuel for our protagonist, the future ice-skating champion. The scene succeeded in being precisely what the director wanted it to be: a humanizing device for young Tonya, foreshadowing the difficult road ahead, both the personal tumult that would define her life and the inspirational foundation for her give-no-fucks fighting spirit. It was a necessary scene for the audience not only to understand her but to like and root for her, to feel her injustices and relate to them. The viewer now knows: Tonya Harding takes shit from nobody. It is the beginning of her redemption. A father leaving his family is not the eye-rolling pathology it is treated as when it occurs in the black community, armchair psychology to explain the plight of the poor. It is turned, by the miracle of film and sympathetic storytelling, into an asset.

A general suspension of disbelief is required when attending any film. The director (in this case Gillespie) asks viewers to accompany him on a journey of his vision. Once the viewer chooses to no longer participate with the director, the movie fails. A few years earlier, in 2015, the veteran African American director Antoine Fuqua released *Southpaw*, a story about a white light-heavyweight boxer whose ascent is followed by a spectacular fall and rehabilitation. Fuqua made a pragmatic, cynical choice: he told a story about the more commonly black and brown boxing world with a white lead, Jake Gyllenhaal. Even his character's name—Billy Hope—is a historical nod to the racism of not just the sport but the audience, which for decades, from the time of Jack Johnson to Gerry Cooney in the 1980s, desperately sought a Great White Hope to put the uppity black champion in his place. Boxing is a black and brown game. In Hollywood, where audiences require whiteness for virtue—the *Rocky* franchise–extending *Creed* films starring Michael B. Jordan being the outlier—it is a white one.

Gyllenhaal's character is the only white fighter in the movie, and in the real world, boxing hasn't had a white American light-heavyweight champion since Bobby Czyz in 1987. Yet, the formula was the same as in *I, Tonya*: Hollywood made the decision that the story of a white fallen champion would produce the type of sympathy a protagonist requires. Where there is black dignity in films like these, it appears in the form of the stereotypical "magical Negro," committed to the redemption of the white lead. In the case of *Southpaw*, that responsibility falls to Forest Whitaker.

Would the story of a black champion who loses everything and commits to rebuilding his life appeal to the white ticket buyer? The public will never know because no one in Hollywood was willing to take that chance. Even an experienced, well-respected director like Fuqua did not feel he could get such a film made.

Hollywood was convinced that Tonya Harding's chainsmoking pugnacity would reach audiences, and it was in these early moments of *I, Tonya* that I watched the construction of her biographical sketch: poverty framed as adversity to overcome, obstacle forged into motivation, even virtue, and I could not help but feel embittered by the care taken with white poverty. When poor Tonya feels inadequate because the snooty skating girls wear fur coats to the rink, her not-yet-deadbeat dad hunts some rabbit for a makeshift, rancid fur coat for his little angel. Poverty requires resourcefulness.

There was pride in their being "white trash" and the audience, one could see, grew to like and respect the spunky warrior from the other side of the tracks, with her blond ponytail and blue eyes, braces, cigarettes, and empty wallet. One could feel the audience see themselves in her, in that uniquely American delusion: no handouts, no complaints. Deal with the shitty hand you were dealt. An obvious mythology, considering the statistics that show white people receiving government assistance in higher numbers than blacks, and respect was the storytelling device rarely afforded black poverty, which is treated as hopeless, its victims comfortable within that hopelessness—and utterly without resources.

The watchful eye of the camera always intently focused on the dangers of the ghetto, not the dignity and fight that comes with surviving it, even though Stevie Wonder gave it voice in 1973 on *Innervisions*. Black Pride. Black Dignity. No handouts. Deal with the hand given you. "Her clothes are old," Stevie sang on "Living for the City," "but never are they dirty." Many black parents know firsthand that life isn't fair and prepare their children to face the world knowing such. Head up. No complaints. With an added layer: if you *do* survive the poverty, remember to be three times as good as the white people against whom you will soon compete.

Yet black poverty on film, through white eyes, rarely contains dignity or virtue or drive. Poverty is never humanized. It is in that spirit that Craig Gillespie depicts Tonya Harding's poverty triumphantly, sympathetically, an obstacle unfairly placed by life at her doormat, barricading her, impeding her progress, shaping her worldview—and dammit, Tonya was gonna find a way. It was in that spirit that I watched this entertaining film of a conniving woman and bumbling men with a darkening mood.

None of the film's themes was revelatory. On screen or in media, white rehabilitation is no new phenomenon. School shooters become troubled lone wolves. Dirty basketball players are rebranded as *intense*. Dishonored, lawbreaking figure skaters are redeemed. Why did watching the same, predictable tropes anew force me to question why I was even in the theater?

It was precisely that, the predictability of the tropes, their rehabilitative intentions, and the consideration of the publishing, broadcast, and Hollywood labyrinth that ends with some projects greenlit, on screens across the country. The stories that sit on the desks or in the bottom of the wastebaskets of agents and executives tell different stories, or the same stories but without the humanizing. Some stories are greenlit. Most are kindling.

I, Tonya was ostensibly disconnected from politics but it was released in the middle of a torrent and it was impossible to watch the themes and the characters without thinking about the America unfolding outside the theater walls. A message, however unintentional, was being sent through this story that virtue belonged to the white working class—even when the protagonist was not only a disgrace but a criminal. *I, Tonya* was released ten months after the Trump inauguration and its reassertion of America as exclusively white. And it came out just two months after the Charlottesville white supremacy rally that left Heather Heyer murdered and Trump referring to the torch carriers who marched through town chanting "Jews will not replace us" as "very fine people." The film appeared with America in the midst of a mood that, after eight years of a black president, white values would be restored.

It was through the lens of whiteness that *I, Tonya* transformed from kinda, sorta quirky and weird to grotesque, made even more so because there was a time when Tonya Harding was demonized because of her class in comparison to her victim, America's sweetheart, Nancy Kerrigan. As valuable as it may be to reappraise the cruelty that came with being villainized for being poor, Harding's rehabilitation, her chance to look into America's face without remorse, regret, or admission and say, "You did this to me," was inevitable. *I, Tonya* was not the first reappraisal giving Harding the floor, but at least the third, preceded by two 2014 documentaries: ESPN's *The Price of Gold*, part of its 30 for 30 series, and NBC's *Tonya and Nancy: The Inside Story*. Both reassessed Harding through the lens of class stigma as working-class whiteness reasserted itself. Even after pleading guilty to obstructing justice, her protagonist moment awaited. She only needed to bide her time.

White outrage post-Trump took on different characteristics, and perhaps Harding's restoration might have felt different had it not come after a campaign of restorative whiteness (had it ever required restoration?). Theatergoers received their illusory uplift. Their roots. Their pride. George Bush, Hillary Clinton,

Donald Trump—Ivy Leaguers, all—attempting to connect with coal miners and the trailer-park waitresses of the *I, Tonya* variety to show they are really alike. The film was an ugly counter to all those blacks and browns for whom surviving poverty carries only fault and blame and shame and the ridicule of requiring government assistance, the dreaded "handout." Given the political climate surrounding the release of *I, Tonya*, the tropes were especially infuriating. They wanted me to care about Tonya Harding, but really, I didn't.

EASY ANSWERS

In 2017, before the biggest games of his life, it was revealed that Luke Heimlich, an all-world pitcher for Oregon State University, the Pac-12 Conference pitcher of the year, was a convicted sex offender. Heimlich had pled guilty to having sex with a female cousin when he was fifteen. His sexual contact with the young girl, he admitted, began when she was four years old and continued until she was six. Heimlich's record was sealed but a clerical error placed his name in a database of convicted sex offenders who had failed to register. At the time, Heimlich was the star pitcher for a team in the College World Series. Though the university allowed him to remain enrolled in school, he withdrew from the team. He was also expected weeks later to be selected in the Major League Baseball amateur draft, laying the foundation for the multimillionaire's good life of big-league baseball. After the revelations were made public, the draft came and went. No team selected Heimlich.

The next year, when Heimlich went 15–1 and was named NCAA pitcher of the year and again received no interest from pro teams, *Sports Illustrated* sent one of its best writers, S. L. Price, to Oregon—the same territory as Tonya Harding—for an extensive cover story that appeared May 21, 2018. The cover photo of Heimlich, wearing his OSU cap and jersey, was flanked by words.

Above his head: *THERE ARE TWO LUKE HEIMLICHS TO CONSIDER . . .*

To the right of him:

THE FIRST is the Luke who admitted to committing the most abhorrent of crimes in his youth, a teenage sex offender who has paid his societal debt and thought his case would never become public.

THE SECOND Luke wants this on the record: "I pled guilty. But ever since that day and even before that, in court records and everything I've denied ever committing that offense. I stand by that."

Luke Heimlich is one of the country's best college pitchers, a first-round draft pick if judged on talent alone. Will Major League teams reconcile the two Lukes, as Oregon State has? Will they even try?

This is a story about crime and punishment and the meaning of second chances.

THIS IS A SPORTS STORY WITH NO EASY ANSWERS

Like Tonya Harding, Luke Heimlich was given the floor, on a national stage, to tell his story and say he did not do what he legally confessed to doing. He was allowed to be defiant despite his guilt. He was given a pathway toward humanity—with his words, on his terms. No one in the story recanted their testimony. The state did not conclude that Heimlich's guilt, determined through the science of DNA testing and additional evidence, was suddenly in question. He was the center of a story that was framed around his redemption *all because he said so.* That was enough to question the legal system and our collective morality. He was humanized into a social dilemma.

One source in the profile, a Division I baseball coach, asked, "What's the kid supposed to do now? Kill himself? I have a lot of professional baseball friends who swear they're not going to touch him. . . . I mean, he can't go to Japan. No independent team is going to sign him. No pro team is going to draft him. What's he supposed to do?"

Their worlds could not have been more different, but it was impossible to read the vexed, thoughtful story of Luke Heimlich and not consider the dismissive, incurious treatment of Colin Kaepernick. While Heimlich pleaded guilty to an unspeakable crime yet found a pathway for rehabilitation in his chosen field, Kaepernick was banished from the NFL despite not having broken the law.

Kaepernick received no wrenching profiles about morality, or the NFL's lack of it for banishing him, or the place of police in society, or the legitimacy of second chances, even though the league is peppered with reclamation projects who've been involved in everything from alcoholism to drug abuse to manslaughter, child abuse to domestic violence. Kaepernick's mere presence shattered the cliché of second chances because he had done nothing that justified his first chance being taken from him.

Heimlich and Harding were viewed societally, their chroniclers with the pen and lens offering the public a new angle, something to consider about them as people, something that would give them value and perhaps, through that reappraisal, a second chance.

Throughout his ordeal, Kaepernick was viewed only through the cold lens of business, which is the only way black athletes have historically been seen. The questions about Kaepernick were based off his value to the balance sheet: *Could he still play? Would he be a "distraction" to the team? Would fans come to watch him? Was he responsible for the NFL's ratings (only if they were poor)? Had Nike taken a bad risk on him financially? Was it a financial stroke of genius when the company's stock skyrocketed after his ad campaign?*

He was not a person. He was a business asset, a risk/reward calculation for the balance sheet.

Sports and sports media reflect the attitude of the American mainstream. They reflect the dominant culture, the middle of the road. By whom and what it covers, media also steers the culture, suggesting to it what values it should embrace.

When Kaepernick was applauded for his courage, the honors appeared from outside of sports and from the predictable political freedom fighters: the ACLU, Amnesty International, the NAACP, the academics and the activists, the students and artists, entities that already often found themselves on the fringes of the mainstream. Within the media of his universe, his cause was not treated as a societal issue that required reassessment. He was treated as an un-American subversive who got what he deserved. Even his support was less about him, and even less about his actual adversary, which was policing in America, than it was about parrying the recklessness of Donald Trump.

Through the comparative, compassionate treatment of a person who sexually abused his six-year-old cousin and was convicted for it, the message being sent was that Luke Heimlich, troubled human being, was more deserving of reconsideration than Colin Kaepernick, business consideration, problem, distraction.

Heimlich was framed through the lens of rehabilitation, of what a society does with its criminally disgraced—and what it should do. The enormous salaries and celebrity elevation of professional athletics have made it impossible for Heimlich, thus far, to be drafted by a Major League Baseball team and enter a field where the *minimum* annual salary is nearly $600,000—even if that salary simply happened to be the going rate of his given profession. Would society demand a registered sex offender who happened to be a $12-per-hour desk clerk be denied a living? It is an appropriate, human question, in part answered when the *Sports Illustrated* profile revealed that eleven registered sex offenders attend classes at Oregon State.

S. L. Price is one of the nation's most accomplished sportswriters and asking the societal questions posed by Heimlich's presence is an example of real journalism. Professional sports is just that, a profession. Its salaries, unfortunately, make it a privilege, one the culture deemed Heimlich no longer deserved.* Yet there are likely convicted sex offenders working in every industry in America, just as there are domestic abusers and former convicts, recovering alcoholics and drug addicts. Price told a story he and his employers rightfully determined was worth telling.

Why, exactly, is the Kaepernick story, with all of its complexities and societal questions, *not* worth telling, except through the lens of business? How has it come to be that the collusion among the NFL and its business partners, law enforcement, and the military is not a story? Why is it not of particular importance that the NFL, which profits daily from the images of freedom and democracy, is among the least committed practitioners of those values? The stories that aren't told fail to reach the public not because they are unimportant but precisely because they are. In this case, the reason, of course, is that to the possessors of the lens and the pens, the police are always the protagonists. Another unwritten rule played itself out as well: it was more permissible for people to break the law and find their way back than for black people to challenge it.

To answer these questions with any honesty is to indict whiteness and its historical, foundational illegitimacy. The winners are again telling the story, telling the public who deserves the sympathetic lens and who does not. Having the courage to tell a different story would risk venturing into frightening, uncharted space: the great leap from propaganda, at long last, toward the truth.

* Postscript: Heimlich signed a contract with the Lamigo Monkeys of the Chinese Professional Baseball League, but public outcry over his criminal record prevented him from playing. In the spring of 2019, he was signed by the Tecolotes de los Dos Laredos of the Mexican League. He made his debut April 9, 2019.

3. OPEN SEASON

THE MEDIOCRE WHITE BOY

It has never failed to make me laugh that Vice President Mike Pence refers to his wife, who is three years older than he, as "Mother." The laughter reflects my own particular sense of humor, and also the fact that Mike Pence refers to his wife as "Mother."

In a March 2017 *Washington Post* profile, Karen Pence is called her husband's "prayer warrior." Once, while he spoke with reporters, she did what any dutiful mother would do: she stood silently nearby holding a silver tray of cookies. When he was Indiana governor, she gave him a red telephone as a gift, which he had installed at the statehouse. Only she had the number. The profile also revealed that Pence did not dine alone with women who were not his wife, an edict that originated with Billy Graham but would become known as the "Pence Rule."

Then came the moment when Pence and Mother weren't so funny. As the #MeToo movement intensified, fueled by NBC broadcaster Matt Lauer harassing female coworkers and buying them dildos as gifts; CBS/PBS deep thinker Charlie Rose walking around naked in front of female assistants; and Harvey Weinstein and Bill Cosby descending from moguls to alleged (and in Cosby's case, convicted) sex offenders, so many other ostensibly male right thinkers—some of whom I like to call friends—decided the only way to protect themselves from career-destroying sexual harassment accusations wasn't to be professional and simply refrain from masturbating in front of female coworkers (as the comedian Louis C. K. admitting to doing) but to adopt the Pence Rule.

Many said they were reluctant to resort to such extremes but the acidic combination of the women and the times left them no choice. To clarify: powerful men abuse and assault women in the workplace; Charlie Rose walked around his female assistants without clothes in a professional environment; Cosby was accused of drugging actresses, sixty claims in all. Disgraced CBS executive Les Moonves allegedly canceled Cybill Shepherd's television show because she would not sleep with him, and in response many men concluded from this carnage that instead of standing with their humiliated female colleagues they needed to be protected from them.

The actors in this drama betrayed a profound intellectual dishonesty. In many instances these exchanges sounded not too dissimilar from racial conversations, where the dominant group, white people, refused to see their basic culpabilities, opting instead to engage in that fruitless search for any explanation except to confront American racism directly. (See: anxiety, economic.) The men who adopted a similar position to explain why it was *necessary to protect themselves in today's climate* found themselves unwilling to distill their concern: either they believed a substantial number of women in the workplace—A quarter? Half? A plurality?—were actively plotting to engineer false sexual harassment charges against men or knew they were incapable of coexisting with women without making sexual advances toward them. If the men were not trying to get into their coworker's pants and also believed their female colleagues weren't irrationally conniving to destroy them, then no danger would exist. There is no third way.

Yet very few men (the actor Idris Elba, who said navigation was difficult only if you "have something to hide," was a notable exception) have summoned the courage to admit to these options—or even explore them. In most public examples, men have generally rejected both scenarios as naturally preposterous, even as they continue to lament the perils of a suddenly unsure world where even a friendly smile risks career catastrophe. "I won't even say 'Merry Christmas' to a woman for fear it will be misconstrued," a fellow journalist gravely told me.

In the spirit of "punching down" at the very people who are suffering the injustice, instead of "punching up" at the ones doing the administering, a 2019 *Harvard Business Review* piece titled "The #MeToo Backlash" profiled a 2018 University of Houston study led by Leanne Atwater that concluded, "In the wake of #MeToo, many people expected men to become more reluctant to engage with women at work in certain ways—even though such activities can be crucial for advancement. (A follow-up survey in 2019 showed that the backlash was even worse than anticipated.)" In Atwater's study, "Looking Ahead: How What We Know about Sexual Harassment Now Informs Us of the Future," 5 percent of men admitted to having harassed a colleague, another 20 percent said "maybe" they had, but 41 percent thought men in general would be "more reluctant" to have a one-on-one meeting with women with no others present.[1] Fifty-seven percent of women thought men would. They know.

Nevertheless, whether it is the men who live in fear that to-morrow will be the day they are exposed for trying to kiss the intern at the awards banquet twenty years ago, their coworkers who are proud of having a clear conscience and the Right Politics, or the women who laugh at the jokes and are even harder on fellow women to prove they can make it on the boys' turf without calling human resources every fifteen minutes, the sentiment remains that women lie secretly in wait to revenge-torch the careers of their male coworkers. It remains despite overwhelming data to the contrary, statistical and anecdotal, despite the lack of frivolity in so many allegations. It remains within men. It remains within women. (The "Women for Kavanaugh" placards during Brett Kavanaugh's 2018 Supreme Court confirmation will not soon be forgotten.) It remains despite its moral bankruptcy, and it remains even as the numbers of prominent men revealed as sexual harassers continues to rise, and it remains even as at least seventeen women, as of July 2019, have accused Donald Trump, the sitting president, of sexual assault. Trump debased the presidency by legitimizing Pence, Kavanaugh, and the persistent attitude that the powerful are under the most threat. "It is a very scary time for young men in America," Trump said on October 2, 2018. A similar sentiment has permeated the white mood for the better part of the past four decades, visible in exit polls, attitudes, and litigation: it is harder to be white in America.

THE NEUTRAL ARBITERS

The term "the best defense is a good offense" is one of those rare clichés whose application is more appropriate outside its realm of origin. In sports, teams or players with tremendous offensive capabilities that don't play defense eventually lose. Ask Mike D'Antoni in basketball, John Isner in tennis, or Chip Kelly in football. Even their best offense won't be good enough often enough. In sports, the cliché loses, defeated by its more historically accurate rival *defense wins championships.*

Outside of sports, however, or more specifically in politics and in cultural perception, the cliché works. Repeating a position, even when (or *especially* when) it is untrue, with the intention of it becoming embedded into dialogue or becoming an effective filibuster to the truth, is difficult to overcome. So much time will be spent debunking a heavily repeated untruth that the public, busy with work, parent-teacher conferences, and *Game of Thrones*, eventually will stop seeking the truth. The opposition, meanwhile, will find itself spending so much time on the defensive that it will never have a chance to redirect. The battering of the public with a false position is the cornerstone of misinformation, the base layer of propaganda.

Politically, it's an odious winner. The attack phrase "identity politics" is so overwhelming that, despite its obvious inaccuracies, defense cannot beat offense. It now ascribed only to the minorities, the women, the transgender, the others. Like the dreaded "fake news," it is so ubiquitous that even people whom the term insults use it. White men use "identity politics" as a bludgeon, to remain on the offensive, branding the rest of the electorate as emotional while securing for themselves the default position of neutrality and *reason*. While the rest of the public in their various factions are positioned as incapable of seeing beyond their personal characteristics, it is white men who treat themselves as reasonable.

It is a spectacular con, as if being a white man was not in and of itself an identity. In America, being a white man is *the* identity of power, status, luxury, control, and respectability. Yet no matter how much defense to reroute the narrative is employed by politicians, academics, pundits, or barstool experts, it is never quite successful, quite likely because it is the white men who are overwhelmingly in front of the camera and the microphone and on the laptops. The label sticks but only in one direction. Only the left-leaning, the black, the women, or the queer voted or acted based on what it saw in the mirror. In July 2019, the Brennan Center for Justice released a report stating that thirteen US states have never in their history seated a person of color as a state supreme court justice, and though white men make up less than one-third of the country's population, 56 percent of the state supreme court justices in the US were white men.[2] The white man was clear-eyed and level-headed. His identity did not factor into his decision-making. He was blind justice. He was reasonable.

The spectacular nature of the con is amplified by the volume of occupations that hire women or minorities in positions only where one is needed. In sports, black receivers who can run forty yards in 4.2 seconds can be covered only by defensive backs, a position also overwhelmingly black, who can do the same. In publishing, doors are so often closed to women and writers of color who want to write about "neutral" subjects because their value stems only from their unique racialized or gendered experience. The end result becomes the ultimate lose-lose: women and minorities are hired in positions specifically because of their identities, then castigated by white men for expressing them. As Willie Randolph, the great Yankees second baseman, once told me, "No one talks to me about baseball. They only ask me about race, then accuse me of playing the race card."

Only the white man could be trusted to be neutral in a world of partisan hysteria and safe spaces. Go back, for a moment, to September 2018, when the *New Yorker* writer Ben McGrath profiled a new sports show called *On the Clock*. The show aired on Conservative Review Television, a new startup streaming network hosted by Steve Deace and Curt Schilling. In the years following his retirement from baseball, few athletes have been as outwardly political as Schilling, who was suspended by ESPN for his attacks on Muslims and transgender people. He once said Hillary Clinton belonged "under a jail." His social media feed is unflinchingly partisan. A Republican, he is a racist and though he may argue the label, he does not hide this fact. Schilling was employed by the alt-right website *Breitbart*, run at one point by the white nationalist Steve Bannon. He is combative politically, publicly fighting with Democratic politicians and media members alike, and often blames his to-date unsuccessful Baseball Hall of Fame candidacy on his conservative politics. He made frequent claims that he would challenge Elizabeth Warren for her US Senate seat from Massachusetts in 2018—until it was time to show up and run.

Deace's politics are equally unambiguous. He has written for the *Conservative Review* and the right-wing *Washington Times* and is the author of several politically themed books that do not pretend to be anything but right-wing Christian.

Neither Deace nor Schilling has ever made a secret of the identity of his politics, and yet McGrath and his so-smart, liberal magazine, against all available evidence, portrayed the pair of white men as neutral. McGrath noted in his first paragraph that a voiceover to start the show says *On the Clock* aims to "make sports great again." The paraphrase is also part of the headline: "Curt Schilling and Steve Deace Try to 'Make Sports Talk Great Again.'" The story is accompanied by a photograph of Schilling wearing a Donald Trump "Make America Great Again" hat with a "TRUMP" campaign banner in the background. Under the photo is a caption of Schilling that says, without irony, that he "views the show as a response to a wearingly politicized state of mainstream sports talk."

"The premise," McGrath writes straightforwardly of the show, "is that sports talk, as brought to you by the mainstream media—especially ESPN, Schilling's former employer—has become tiresomely politicized, and restoring its greatness involves embracing the attitudes of a time 'before everybody decided sports was boring and everything was racist,' as Deace says." Deace is quoted by McGrath using political dog whistles such as "socialistic" and derogatory terms like "snowflakes." And yet, at no point during the profile is either defined as a political ideologue, or their show as being as politically partisan as the positions they oppose. The profile uses Trump-speak throughout. If it is attempting irony or subtlety it fails miserably, for McGrath is direct in his description of the show's premise but meekly indirect in its deconstruction (ignoring completely mentioning Schilling's firing from ESPN for his racism). Even in a liberal publication—or especially in one—the white men were going to bring balance to an ostensibly politically imbalanced sports world. They were going to restore order. They were going to be reasonable.

INTERLUDE: WHEN BLACK PEOPLE PRACTICE WHITE SUPREMACY

Once, after playing tennis, I ordered sushi takeout. I took a bite of mackerel nigiri and felt a significant crunch, as if I'd bitten into a pebble. Mackerel is soft and certainly not crunchy. I rolled the hard item around in my mouth and, growing more horrified, spit out my food. I look down at what appeared to be . . . yes . . . a tooth.

There was a fucking tooth in my sushi!

I was nauseous. I was horrified. I was dialing the number of the restaurant to tell them how quickly I would see them in court—but only after the board of health shut them down. In mid-dial, I ran my tongue along the bottom right side of my mouth and felt a smooth space, a divot.

Wait . . . oh no . . . it's mine. It's my own tooth.

I hung up quickly.

I grind my teeth. Once I ground them so hard I cracked the back right molar. The dentist had tried to keep it together with a crown. It appeared I cracked the crown during my tennis match, clenching too hard while serving. The crown fell out, winding up in my mackerel.

While I was sitting in the dentist's chair, my highly recommended oral surgeon, who was going to perform the root canal I now needed, entered. He looked at me and introduced himself. I looked at him with caution and disbelief. He was tall, professional, and . . . *black.*

Black professionals know the look. I have received it too many times, that millisecond it takes to readjust, to recalibrate to the disbelief that your doctor or lawyer or white-collar professional is black. He doesn't look the part. He is in a space he doesn't belong. For as long as I've had teeth my oral surgeons have all been white or Middle Eastern. My dentists have been white men, Asian men, and Asian women. My dental hygienists have all been white women.

Black professionals know the difference in the look when they receive it from another black person. Most times it is a welcome, periodically jarring surprise. In other cases, the presence of a black professional produces distrust. The black lawyer, author, doctor, or oral surgeon cannot be as competent as their white counterparts.

It was a fleeting impulse but it was there.

If not a momentary skepticism of his credentials, then a surprise at his presence. Perhaps they are the same thing. He didn't look the part, and questioning even for a moment his competence never would have entered my mind had a white man shown up in his lab coat because that is what an oral surgeon is supposed to look like. He would have been another white man in an occupation where white men live. He might have been patently mediocre but he looked the part.

Numerous black professionals have expressed frustration to me about being routinely rejected by skeptical whites and especially by suspicious blacks for not looking the part. A black financial planner I know finds more difficulty attracting black clients because he senses their hesitation to trust a black money manager. "So, they'll put their money in Bernie Madoff's hands and let him steal from them because he's white, but they don't trust me," he told me. I recall an optometrist openly remarking, "I would have never thought that by looking at you," when I told him I was a journalist. Gary Washburn, a basketball writer for the *Boston Globe*, once told me he has seen several book collaborations fail to materialize because black athletes subconsciously or actively favor white writers, who represent the mainstream and appear more *legitimate*.

"Children of movie stars, like white people, have at—or actually in—their fingertips an advantage that is genetic. Because they are literally the progeny of movie stars they look specifically like the movie stars who have preceded them, their parents. They don't have to convince us that they can be movie stars," Fran Leibowitz wrote in a 1997 *Vanity Fair* essay on race. "We take them instantly at face value. Full face value. They look like their parents, whom we already know to be movie stars. White people look like their parents, whom we already know to be in charge. This is what white people look like—other white people. The people in charge. That's the advantage of being white. And that's the game. So by the time the white person sees the black person standing next to him at what he thinks is the starting line, the black person should be exhausted from his long and arduous trek to the beginning."

IN THE NAME OF DIVERSITY

Imagine for a moment that the trek to the beginning was not met with collective triumph that America was meeting its promise but with total contempt, and that the journey of being twice as good—of joining the lost tribe—ended with the privilege of standing next to people who simply look the part. Those white people believe completely in their legitimacy, that they belong wherever they happen to be standing, and the public requires little more than the looks of their faces to be comforted by them. Imagine being the person, as the saying goes, who was born on third base but thinks he hit a triple—and being considered worthy of gaining the base. Imagine also being inundated for a lifetime with the rhetoric of meritocracy, working hard, pulling oneself up, calling oneself self-made, and recognizing, finally and painfully, that your black presence is not the triumph of the level playing field but the center of total resentment. Black people in the white-collar trades need not imagine very hard. They live it and know that more effort has gone into maintaining the protections that white men have gotten for looking the part than into ensuring merit. The diversity workshops and company directives and inclusivity seminars sound encouraging but their very necessity explains to the black employee the corporate landscape better than any human resources spin doctor ever could: while merit is treated as a natural recognition of ability, an entire corporate initiative is required to recognize you at all.

In the early to mid-1990s newspaper business, greater attention was being paid not only to the stories being told but to who was allowed to tell them. A common lament was heard in newsrooms and press boxes around the country: white reporters returning from unsuccessful job interviews claimed they were being passed over in favor of minorities—in the name of diversity. It was constantly repeated by white reporters even when the numbers did not support them, and while companies may have directed their managers to include a diverse pool of applicants, it was still the kingmakers, the white male editors, actually making the hires.

I remember a moment of peak frustration after hearing yet another white man complain to me he couldn't get ahead while suggesting the fix was in against him. I naturally, was the fix, for the implication was that editors were being told to hire black reporters instead of *good* reporters. I was standing near the back of the Fenway Park press box looking at the rows of white male writers, the first two rows in front of me and two more behind. Many of them were colleagues with whom I'd shared beers and tall tales—and who believed and repeated often that diversity was eradicating their livelihoods. In 2018 the *Columbia Journalism Review* reported that the *New York Times*' reporting team for the 2016 political season was 90 percent white and *USA Today*'s was 83 percent white. According to the 2018 Associated Press Sports Editors Racial and Gender Report Card, 85 percent of sports editors and 80.3 percent of sports columnists in America were white. As the only black person in the press box that day, I said loudly, "I thought black people were taking all the jobs?" A few looked up. Some gave a knowing *touché*. Others gave an eye roll. Everyone went back to work.

Recalling that day in the press box and so many others like them, when competitors and colleagues alike were convinced they were self-made, always returned me to Leibowitz's essay. "And what it is like to be white is not to say, 'We have to level the playing field,'" she continued, "but to acknowledge that not only do white people own the playing field but they have so designated this plot of land as a playing field to begin with. White people *are* the playing field. The advantage of being white is so extreme, so overwhelming, so immense that to use the word 'advantage' at all is misleading since it implies a kind of parity that simply does not exist."

THE ASSUMPTION OF COMPETENCE

Just as America's fetishizing of police provides the misdirection for its true aim of protecting whiteness, fear of being called into human resources for making a drunken comment to a co-worker during a long-ago Christmas party is not the primary rationale for men believing in the Pence Rule. Nor is it credible that with so much physical, obvious evidence to the contrary, white people really believe minorities assume a preponderance of jobs. In the history of the NBA, the supposed hallmark of black athletic success where 80 percent of the players are black, there have been just ten black coaches in the league's seventy-three-year history who were *not* former players. This means that the average black coach has virtually no chance to be hired in the NBA, for unlike his average white counterpart, the over-whelming majority of black coaching aspirants must first possess the world-class ability to reach the NBA as a player, a talent an infinitesimal percent of the world's black population possesses. It is an impossible barrier. In the history of the league, which dates to 1946, there have been two—*two*—black majority own-ers and the first one, Robert Johnson, sold his franchise to the second, Michael Jordan. The NFL went sixty-nine years without a black head coach and the reason that ended wasn't the sudden recognition in 1989 that Art Shell was a rare football genius, but because two high-profile sports figures—the CBS broad-caster Jimmy "the Greek" and Los Angeles Dodgers executive Al Campanis—were fired for making racist comments publicly regarding the competency of black job candidates. Sports did not recognize meritocracy. They were responding to pressure.

When they are hired, black head coaches in the NFL are fired notoriously quickly. Neither the NFL nor MLB has ever approved a black-majority owner. Baseball, where to even have a shot at being a manager first required being a terrific player, embodies the *twice as good* edict. Established in 1869, Major League Baseball has hired fifteen black men to manage teams.

Nine have been former All-Stars and three (Frank Robinson, Don Baylor, and Maury Wills) were former MVPs. The black players in baseball used to repeat the saying, "No blacks on the bench." That meant that if baseball was going to admit black players, they had to be starter-level good.

None of this, it should be noted, is anything new. In the years before baseball integration in the 1940s the black players taking the white man's job—which he acquired not through merit but exclusion—was the great fear. That, and a fear of competition. "The Negro players have eliminated the marginal white player," San Francisco Giants manager Alvin Dark said in a 1964 interview. "Those good colored boys have run all those fine white boys to the mound where there is not that much competition."

This is an example of Leibowitz's "arduous trek to the beginning." Black players were first challenged to overcome segregation on the field, for it wasn't their lack of ability that kept baseball, football, and basketball white for decades but white edict. In the fifty-plus years since black coaches entered the ranks (Bill Russell of the Boston Celtics became the first black head coach in professional sports in 1967), they have had to overcome not looking the part without the weapon of superior speed or quickness. In baseball, no black manager has been hired who was not a former player at the big-league level and half never received a second opportunity after being fired. In the NFL, two-thirds of the black coaches who have been hired have never received a second opportunity. They are the original One and Done.*

The *New York Times*, established in 1851, has had two black general sports columnists in its history, neither of them women.

---

* Fifteen black men have been hired as manager in the history of Major League Baseball. One, Dave Roberts of the Los Angeles Dodgers, remains with his original team and thus has not yet had the chance to be hired by another team. The same is true in the NFL of Pittsburgh's Mike Tomlin. Thus, though the NFL has had twenty-one black head coaches, thirteen of the nineteen who have been fired never received another opportunity.

The *Boston Globe* has hired two full-time black sports colum-nists, the *Boston Herald* and *San Francisco Chronicle* each has had only one, and dozens of others have not had any. When he was a player, Charles Barkley once said, "Every time you talk to a group of reporters, you're talking to ninety-nine white guys and one black guy pretty much every day of your life."

Both the #MeToo movement and diversity initiatives threaten the kingdom of male mediocrity, particularly white male mediocrity. There has been, essentially, one area in sports where black talent is vital and that area is on the field when black players are clearly the superior physical choice, such as speed po-sitions in the NFL or most NBA positions. If there is a job that either a white or black person can perform—like, say, coaching or writing or evaluating—the doors are often limited or closed completely for black people.

The same is true when it comes to gender. Filling the breach are white women. Left out are black women. Our common language ensures this, creating for white women an exclusive lane, the carpool lane of diversity. "Women and people of color" really means "white women and everybody else." There is a belief that the progressive NBA is comfortable with the game being overwhelmingly black in style, culture, and demographic and that the NFL is comfortable being 70 percent black. The opposite is closer to the truth. The game is comfortable with black talent playing but has never been comfortable with black coaches and commentators who were not former players. Black people know they've always been allowed to entertain whites but without much opportunity after the final buzzer. The racial hierarchy of sports has gone largely unchanged for a century:

White owners.
White coaches.
White media.
White season-ticket buyers.
Black players.

White women provide the balm for sports that need diversity but must not risk being seen by white audiences as "too black," lest the viewers retreat. On television the formula is as obvious as the Packer Sweep: a white woman hosting with three black ex-players on a panel, or with two black ex-players and a fired white coach who is using television to remain relevant, as a way station for his next job. In addition to show hosts, those sideline reporters who are not white men are mostly white women, as are newspaper columnists and beat reporters. White men dominate the sports radio airwaves, and when paired with an African American voice, it is usually a black male ex-player. In diversity studies and profiles, black women are rarely mentioned. Is it to be accepted that black women have nothing unique to add to commentary, news coverage, or a broadcast, that they have no voice of value? Black women are not often considered by the white men who do the hiring because to them, hiring white women has solved the gender issue and hiring black men solves the racial issue. Because sports and corporations in general crave diversity of color but fear diversity of thought, black women are erased without ever really existing.

No alliance is more fragile than that between white and non-white women. Progressive white women weary of men running things and controlling them, who saw the Kavanaugh hearing as the darkest days of their lives, also tire of a persistent, inescapable statistic: 52 percent of white women voted for Donald Trump. As a bloc, white women represent the only demographic uncertainty. Ninety-four percent of black, 83 percent of Asian, and 69 percent of Hispanic women voted for Hillary Clinton.[3] Some white women feel betrayed by their own. Others redirect, refusing blame for votes they did not cast, asking instead why white men are so easily excused for not being better allies. Some of the best writers deal with the subject by not dealing with it at all.

In September 2019, Hasbro released a post-#MeToo, #TimesUp version of the board game Monopoly titled "Ms. Monopoly: The First Game Where Women Make More Than

Men." The star was Mr. Monopoly's niece, a "self-made invest-ment guru." Hasbro trumpeted it as a victory. A black woman friend in the fight found the entire concept of Ms. Monopoly absurd as a tool toward equity, and engaging with a white fe-male coworker she asked, "So, at the end when it all collapses, a woman will be holding all the money? Is that the goal here?"

Her coworker responded, "I'd be okay with that."

White women, alas, remain a powerful second on the Ameri-can food chain of power. They are fluid, able to be friend or foe of both whiteness and patriarchy. They can maintain whiteness, take power for themselves, and consider it success. They can win with or without change. They can simultaneously claim to sup-port diversity while their ascension erases it, oppose patriarchy politically while safely marrying or, in the case of the fictional but metaphorically very real Ms. Monopoly, being born into it. They can say the right things while becoming its heir. They can triumph by defeating patriarchy while leaving the cultural dominance of whiteness intact. Many white women would "be okay with that," their excluded dark-skinned female allies forced to accept such a victory as yet another defeat. This must be confronted.

Clinging to the Pence Rule, now the men don't trust white women, either.

If men believe they cannot trust women not to destroy their careers, what, exactly, are these women gaining for all their con-niving, for their obvious attempts at entrapment? What is their prize? Where is their throne? In sports they gain admittance to a club that does not want them and never has, one that has never in large measure respected their intellect. They get to step on a Major League Baseball field to interview a player, only—as I per-sonally recall one exchange—to have that player wink and say, "I fucked her" as she walked out of earshot. They get to have another player, as I remember personally witnessing, implore a female reporter to come to his locker in the visiting clubhouse in Cleveland because he had something *really important to tell her*, and when she approached he opened his laptop and showed her a porn video of a woman on her knees performing oral sex on two men. As she tried to walk away, the player grabbed her arm and said, "Wait, wait! This is the *good* part." They get, after a 49ers-Eagles game in 1992, during my first year in the business at the *Oakland Tribune*, to have Reggie White, the Eagles' superstar defensive end, emerge from the shower wearing a towel but refuse to address the media until the lone female reporter, Michelle Smith, left the room. The male reporters did not stand up for her, did not allow her the opportunity to do her job. They waited for her to leave and then they asked their questions.

In the press box, women lose. Should a woman break a story, almost without fail she will be accused of having sex with an athlete as the explanation for her success. If women do not break stories (even though most of the mediocre male reporters who surround them also do not), it is considered proof they weren't qualified to have their job in the first place. If they are pretty, they were hired for that reason (and therefore *must* be fucking somebody, right?). If they are not, they are ignored, and weren't likely to advance, anyway.

And they earn less.

What is done with their loss? The men scratch their collective heads—confounded, detached from any personal responsibility—over the fact that so many women appear to have a dream job but wind up leaving the business unfulfilled, even though for generations many of the same head-scratchers were the ones telling them their presence was unwanted. They were offered sympathy but not solidarity because their very presence was a threat to the mediocre white boys who run the industry and now also to the trickle of mediocre black boys who have been granted (temporary) access to the club.

The threat is so great that a woman with a pad and pen cannot be trusted to sit alone in a room with a male coworker or supervisor without witnesses. The threat to men is real but it's not a threat of entrapment. It's a threat to their remaining unchallenged, remaining comfortably mediocre without competition. An unspoken motive of refusing to include women in after-work dinners, individual meetings, and hybrid business-social occasions is to slide them directly out of competition, for it is in those quasi-social settings that promotions and confidences and all the intangibles of the corporate climb really take place. "If I didn't have frequent dinners/drinks with men," the historian Keri Leigh Merritt told me, "I wouldn't have a career."

White men afford themselves the assumption of competence. It is how they protect their position and mediocrity—for in any profession, there are precious few exceptional talents of any race or gender—from competition. As smug in the press box as they are in the front office, the classroom, and the boardroom, they assume their collective competence while assuming the *incompetence* of the black and the female, spending ample time undermining the credentials and professionalism of both. White men often compete with one another for jobs in the press box; some may believe they are the better candidate but rarely, if ever, do they suggest (as they often do with black people) that their white male colleagues are *unqualified* to even be in the profession. At a 2019 diversity seminar hosted by the Federal Reserve Bank of Boston, one of the featured CEOs told an overflow crowd of women and minority professionals that managers often find it easier to promote white men because they know a white man passed over in favor of a minority candidate might create unrest, while black and female candidates are less likely to create a similar stir if they are the ones passed over. These white men assume their own professional qualifications, which justifies their anger at potentially being overlooked for a promotion. They are convinced that only force—via diversity initiatives such as the NFL's Rooney Rule and baseball's Selig Rule, Title IX, and sexual harassment lawsuits—is the only way minorities and women could advance. They assume their own competence. Everyone else arrived via handout and they will not stand for it.

The value of the mediocre white boy to the company cannot

be underestimated. He is a prime asset. He does not complain. He fits in. He doesn't file discrimination lawsuits—unless it is against the black people he feels are taking his God-given job. He has no ambitions and no expectations, and thus is not a problem. And because he looks the part and poses no threat, he and the boys and the bosses can all go to the Irish pub or the strip bar or the game, laugh at the diversity and inclusion seminars, bitch about Dick Lapchick and his race and gender report cards, comply begrudgingly with company directives, and *keep everything intact.*

The Pence Rule as self-protection against #MeToo may sound pragmatic but it is, quite simply, misdirection. It is Hitchcock's MacGuffin. The true aim is to eliminate female competition for jobs—or at least reduce it and make advancement for women more difficult, the work environment for them even more hostile, increasingly isolating them from an industry's social and political nerve centers, punishing them because Louis C. K. couldn't just masturbate in private. Of course, as MacGuffins go, we have been here before, a quarter century ago when the white boys in the press box making jokes about niggers (yes, they used the term blatantly) were suddenly fearful of losing their jobs for making those jokes and their lament was the racial and generational equivalent of refusing to being alone in a room with a female reporter. The world had gotten too *politically correct* and the inability to joke as openly as they had before meant the end of civilization. It wasn't only their world anymore. The formula remains unchanged: diversity means competition and competition threatens mediocrity, and the two combined mean accountability, an end of the white boys' club as it has been known. (Side note: to the black people in the press box who had spent their careers putting up with the insults as part of the job, it was a day long overdue.)

THE HERO GAME

Like the arrival of bottomless French fries, America reached another milestone in depravity on May 31, 2018, when Donald Trump, born to wealth and having reached national fame by being on TV, released a photo of himself sitting behind his Oval Office desk with Kim Kardashian West, born to wealth but having reached fame by being on TV, standing behind him. Lacking credentials and credibility, together these two were going to champion the cause of the criminal justice reform through the case of Alice Marie Johnson, a sixty-three-year-old great-grandmother whose life sentence for a nonviolent drug offense was commuted by Trump after she served twenty-two years.

A week later, television cameras showed Johnson in a grayish sweat suit running toward her family, freed after being sent to prison forever under Bill Clinton's destructive criminal justice policies in 1996, when she was forty-one years old, and denied clemency by Barack Obama in 2016, when she was sixty-one. It was a moment all too common in America: the photo op standing in for justice, fantasy replacing outrage at failed systems and stolen lives, and sports-style scoreboard watching replacing journalism, a seemingly bulletproof moment for Trump, a man who counts success in terms of optic victories instead of actual ones. It was a victory also for Kardashian, who seems convinced that substance is something you can buy, bundled with airtime.

Trump bathed in the attention because attention is all that

matters. The man who had advocated for the execution of drug dealers, for executing the innocent five young men in the infamous 1989 Central Park Five case, had now saved the day, proving he could Get Things Done. He positioned the clemency of Johnson as proof also of his interest in black people despite his lifelong obvious and documented racism. He then immediately indulged in his signature cravenness, turning the lives of 2.2 million incarcerated people in America into a game of clemency roulette ("Who should I pardon next?" he said to the cameras following Johnson's release) before returning to his natural instinct of attacking black people, challenging protesting NFL players to provide him "a list" of people who should be pardoned.

But Alice Johnson was free and America had fallen for the gesture, that collective reflex where the One Good Deed obscures a long résumé of wreckage. No matter the toxicity, America's leaders are a press release away from redemption. Lazy and incurious, the news media covered the entire Alice Johnson charade similarly. It fell for the gesture with Trump, and with Kardashian engaged in the hero game, the surrender of civic engagement in favor of the celebrity class coming to save us, the tax-avoiding cavalry arriving one Ferrari at a time.

Take, for example, a few headlines following Johnson's release:

The *San Diego Union Tribune*: "How Kim Kardashian is Becoming the New Face of Criminal Justice Reform"

The *Las Vegas Journal Review*: "It May Take Kim Kardashian to Spur Criminal Justice Reform"

Real Clear Politics: "Trump Flirts with Pardons and Prison Reform"

AL.com: "Johnson Thanks Trump for 'Having Mercy'"

It was disgusting.

The freeing of Alice Johnson was a wonderful moment—for Alice Johnson. She was free after serving twenty-two unnecessary years in prison, but Kardashian provided the perfect accomplice for Trump's misdirection and America's thirst for the hero narrative. While the cameras flashed and Kardashian spoke of her "mission" to free Johnson—she would later talk about helping more people and even one day perhaps attending law school—the attorney general at the time, Jeff Sessions, had within the first one hundred days of the Trump administration erased an Obama-era directive to end the federal government's partnerships with private prisons, a relationship that incentivized law enforcement to imprison more people—and imprisoning more people means imprisoning more black people. There isn't much point to having a multimillion-dollar contract with firms whose prisons are empty. "Now," according to a report on the Bureau of Prisons from New York University's Brennan Center for Justice, "the BOP is free to continue and expand the use of private prisons, a signal that Sessions expects the prison population to grow."

Alice Johnson appeared on the morning news circuit, thanking Trump for freeing her. She appeared on the *Today* show with Kardashian, who vowed to find even more Alice Johnsons and free them too. For an opiated country, bloated on fast food and offended by facts, she became the heartwarming human interest story of the moment that gave a disinterested America something to feel good about while watching TV at the dentist.

For every other day, however, Sessions was undermining the Obama administration's work to actually reduce the prison population. Even as more than half the states moved to decriminalize or outright legalize marijuana, Sessions sought maximum sentences for marijuana use.

"In its place, they have built a more draconian vision of law enforcement, centered around immigration," the Brennan report wrote of the Trump administration's assault on Obama-era reform. "While many of these changes occurred without drawing public scrutiny, consequences have already begun to materialize in areas such as immigration enforcement. Over the next

three years, these shifts could cause the federal prison population to begin increasing again."

The Trump-Kardashian charade, however, produced its intended effect: the celebrity concierge had delivered an array of
services—to itself. Trump, attacker of black people, especially
of the nation's first black president and its most accomplished
athletes, had a black woman on national television thanking him
for his mercy, and Kardashian won for her brand the title of
the "face" of criminal justice reform. It also revealed America's
embarrassing habit of caring about something only if it is affixed to the shiny object that is celebrity. Some fellow celebrities
defended Kardashian against the criticism that she was overmatched, used by Trump as a pawn while Sessions ruined more
black people.

Meanwhile, America once more chose the celebrity class
over the career professionals who had spent their lives study-
ing public policy. (I mean, what could *they* possibly know? Like,
nobody even knows *their* names.) The cameras flickered and the
real math was being tallied: thousands of people—with a high
likelihood of them being black and poor—subject to harsher and
longer prison terms under Trump and Sessions were being ex-
changed for one Alice Johnson and a morning of TV talk-show
interviews. America was so easily distracted by the bauble of celebrity, it was like putting a squirrel in front of a cocker spaniel.

FALLING IN LOVE WITH THE GESTURE

Since it is so common, so often repeated along such predictable
lines, it was important to ask: What, exactly, is the purpose of
this fantasy? Falling in love with the gesture is one of America's
most beloved pastimes, a ritual of rehabilitation that ignores the
evidence of our situation, the long-term consequence. It offers
the appearance of progress, reconciliation, and reflection while
leaving whole systems and destructive legacies entirely in place.
During one stretch in 2018, it felt like an everyday occurrence.

A week before Alice Johnson became a household name

for exactly twenty-four hours, Donald Trump again sat in the Oval Office surrounded by more celebrities, Sylvester Stallone chief among them. Two others members of the rich and famous flanked him: boxing champions Deontay Wilder and the legendary Hall of Famer Lennox Lewis. The occasion, more than a century in the making, was the presidential pardon of Jack Johnson, the first black heavyweight champion, who navigated the most racist period of the twentieth century by scandalizing it. The scandal of Johnson's story still survives: the white boxers refusing to fight him, his marrying of white women, white America's nationwide search to find a "great white hope" to finally put the nigger champion in his place. In 1920 Johnson served ten months in prison for violating the White Slave Traffic Act, also known as the Mann Act, which prohibited the transporting of a white woman across state lines for "immoral purposes," a crime for which Johnson had once fled the country. For decades, advocates for both Johnson and justice petitioned for a pardon. Nearly one hundred years later, with much White House pageantry, the celebrity concierge sprang to action. Stallone called Trump. Trump pardoned Johnson.

A little more than a month earlier, the nation mourned the death of the former first lady Barbara Bush, wife of George H. W. Bush and matriarch of the Bush political dynasty. The coverage of her death centered around one moment that had become her public signature: her March 1989 visit to Grandma's House, a facility that cared for sick children, and the photo of her holding and kissing crying Donovan, an infant stricken with HIV. To the mainstream, the first lady's visit to Grandma's House represented a transformation in the nation's attitudes about the AIDS epidemic. At the time of her death, it was her most humanizing public appearance.

Then near the end of that summer, John McCain, the venerable Arizona senator, died after a long bout with brain cancer. McCain's death occurred in the shadow of an America in combat, around the world and with itself, exemplified by the unstatesmanlike and churlish Trump. At a time of division and classlessness and exposure of America's intractability, McCain had over his final months repositioned himself as both balm to the nation's sunburn and a beacon of respect between citizens amid disagreement. McCain's credentials as an American inspiration, icon, and powerful political figure went unchallenged, and during the weeklong commemoration of his death, he emerged the unifier: as a final request, Trump was not invited to his funeral and McCain's confrontation with a racist supporter following his 2008 loss to Barack Obama was replayed repeatedly as an example of McCain's decency even toward his political opponents. McCain's defense of Obama certified his status as the ultimate country-before-party statesman. Democrats celebrated McCain as if he were one of their own, and this was precisely the point: he was. Everyone was American.

Each of these gestures was hailed as defining the moment. None of them, however, very much served the truth. Through these examples and too many others, it was not difficult to conclude that America were engaging in a certain adolescent fantasy, a Hollywood story that followed the facile script that everyone, when the sand finally runs out of their hourglass, contains some goodness. Nor is it, in the case of McCain or Barbara Bush especially, simply a case of being polite to not speak ill of the dead. Bush hugging the HIV-positive baby softened, if not erased, all of her ideological choices (at least the public policy with which she chose to align herself) over ninety-two long years of life. Those choices unapologetically connected her to power, to whiteness, to conservative principle and theory, and to political policies that, hug or not, genuine in that moment or not, directly guaranteed that that little pandemic-stricken infant had virtually no chance. Upon her death, in 2018, little was said about her *beyond* that gesture, which made her America's First Grandma and bestowed upon her a compassion the policies she supported certainly did not. The hug was completely rehabilitative—to her.

Hugging little Donovan did not create a new political ideology that confronted the devastation of the gay community in America. It did not make the Bush dynasty a political ally to gay Americans who desperately needed advocates, and resources. The Bush dynasty, despite the words of Bono, the reams of paper used for reflections on this heartwarming human moment, continued its political hostility toward the LGTBQ community—and that is what counts. That is legacy. What the gesture did do, however, was provide a smooth, grandmotherly sheen to the woman who was long known as the matriarch of a powerhouse political family that had seen twelve years in the White House as president, another eight as vice president, and nearly a quarter century of governorships in two states by two of her sons. It also did something else: it gave a photo op an undeserved currency when the real power behind forcing the AIDS epidemic into a national priority was the unrelenting desperation and rage of the activist group ACT UP.

The gesture did for the First Lady the same service that walking on the Senate floor in 2017 and saving the Affordable Care Act with a dramatic thumbs-down vote did for John McCain. It was the most important step toward creating for McCain a new truth (which is better known as mythology), away from the partisan political combatant whose teasing moments of political cooperation must be paired with the darker legacy of unleashing Sarah Palin on America, a cynical political move that should never be obscured. The appeal of this reflex is that goodness, if packaged just the right way around just the right issue, will not only produce redemption but can erase a lifetime of action and ideology no matter how contradictory. The rehabilitated figure in the farce that was the Jack Johnson "pardoning" was ostensibly Johnson, but in reality it was Donald Trump. He was desperate in his need to be liked, to adopt some cause that would recast the evidence of his existence: that he is and for the totality of his public life has been a racist, hostile and condescending toward African Americans. He had done what no other president, including the nation's only black one, would do, and he demanded credit for it. His taking ownership of the Johnson story, to be able to say he corrected the record, afforded him the currency he sought. This one gesture represented the long-awaited proof that Trump cared about black people after all. Yet the true rehabilitated figure was not Trump but white America itself, for the gesture of providing some insufficient, posthumous justice to Johnson did nothing for the boxer, who has been dead since 1946. Nor did the pardon succeed in its supposedly intended mission of cleansing Johnson because it was never Jack Johnson who required cleansing. He had done nothing wrong except run afoul of a racist law, which is actually what should have been, and should be, on trial. The Jack Johnson crusade, however, made many well-meaning people feel good about being on the right side of justice and gave some people who have never meant well an opportunity to burnish their own image at no cost.

What is the appeal of such nonsense? Falling in love with the gesture absolves an illiterate, celebrity-absorbed electorate of its responsibilities to educate itself and hold its leaders, and itself, accountable. *Accountability*, alas, is a phrase used only for the poor. Pardoning a decades-dead boxer gives the public cover for being unserious and unengaged. The celebrity culture, which has taken up most of their attention and is so often the aspiration, must have meaning in order to absolve the public of all it does not know about its government and its leaders, and of how little it actually cares. It is also a surrender to the unworkable notion that the exceptionalism of America striving to be *more perfect*, more equal, more just and better—is not so exceptional at all. Recognition that American exceptionalism is fantasy increases the emotional *need* for the gesture to assuage the dark time, to make it more bearable, to give it some hope. Who among the public would not choose to embrace the humanity of the first lady holding a dying infant (young Donovan passed away soon after the famous hug) when the public perception in

1989 was that AIDS could be contracted simply by touching a person infected with the disease?

An America wounded by its decay and feeling hopeless needed the image of a heroic McCain more than his far-more-complicated reality. We fall for the gesture because we need it. America knows it is not up for a fight it believed it had inherently won simply by being American. As it turns out, we are not exceptional at all. We are desperate.

THE HERO GAME

The days darken and the good, well-meaning people of America walk around, almost zombielike, looking at one another with pleading expressions, wondering what happened, as if *what happened* has not *been happening* for the entirety of their lives and the entirety of their parents' lives. The warnings of American culture and the consequences of becoming less literate, less compassionate, more wasteful, more materialistic, and more influenced by corporations have existed since Orwell. Perhaps the stunned and the bewildered did not believe they would live to pay the price of largesse that swelled into gluttony, but Americans certainly welcomed the journey. They embraced it as proof of prosperity, happily accepting bigger Christmas gifts, more money, lower taxes, and less civics, more of the postwar good life. What is driving this collective shock is the sudden reality of the end-of-days conclusion—even though virtually the entire genre of science fiction has been dedicated to the inevitable dystopia. As the eye rolls commence on being lectured about literacy and responsibility, the public may have understood in theory that cultural banality would lead to its emptiness, but somehow, no matter how cool it sounded to reference Big Brother, it did not connect emptiness with authoritarianism. It did not think it applied to them.

Data on global warming or stories on the lethal drinking water in Flint, Michigan, receiving less attention than Kanye West saying stupid things drove good, right-thinking people to repeat phrases that sound knowledgeable ("It's bread and circuses all over again") while conveniently forgetting Juvenal's belief that bread and circuses would one day doom the Roman Empire, and that *you* are now the Roman Empire. It is typically American to reference an ominous historical parallel and not think its disastrous conclusion applies to us. We replace destruction with exceptionalism: it could never happen here.

Falling in love with the gesture embraces a one-time, cleansing performance and Americans do yearn for that one feel-good moment, even from (especially from) people who do not deserve rehabilitation. The country also decided that in a time of corporate greed all it needed was more and bigger gestures, from richer and cooler people. America decided what it needed was the hero game.

The March 4, 2002, cover of *Time* magazine made one such announcement with an immodest cover story that asked, "Can Bono Save the World?" with the subtitle "Don't laugh—the globe's biggest rock star is on a mission to make a difference," which attempted to ground the hyperbole. The photo revealed Bono, opening his jacket (which was lined with a pattern of the American flag) somewhat similarly to Superman and as more than the famous front man of the rock band U2. He was a leader among leaders, seated next to Bill Gates at the World Economic Forum. He was heralded as "Africa's greatest champion." His fame made him formidable, important in ways beyond selling records.

At that moment the hero game was not immediately obvious, for to that point rockers had played benefit concerts for causes for nearly fifty years, from the annual civil rights jazz concerts Jackie and Rachel Robinson hosted at their home in the 1960s to Band Aid and USA for Africa to Live Aid, Farm Aid, and dozens of other charity concerts in the 1980s and 1990s. It certainly was not obvious to anyone who trafficked in the black community, where African American entertainers—the ballplayers and singers, especially—had always been expected to accept a disproportionate amount of the economic burden of not only friends and family but also a community starved by its country.

The *Time* cover was signaling something different from an artist with a cause. Bono wasn't being promoted for a concert. He *himself* was being promoted as a savior, a unique visionary who not only had passion for human rights but was now being paired at panels with the world's elite, the power players who had the resources, or at least the money, to take on global-scale problems. He was a hero.

A new template was being forged. Bono, Bill Gates, Bob Geldof, and their super-rich friends would combine their connections, money, and fame to save the world at a time when public wealth was being privatized. They would merge politics, using their fame to connect to world leaders—Bill Clinton and Bono having lunch in Denver once made national news—who would open doors with their political connections and Make Things Happen. The star power was so irresistible that it seemed there was nothing—from wiping out poverty to ending pandemics—that the super-rich could not accomplish.

Bono revved the hero game into high gear. The celebrity class was the magic elixir. There was *Wired* magazine in 2013 running a very serious-looking cover with very two serious-looking men sitting at a round table. One was Gates. The other was Clinton. The cover story headline read "Bill Gates Wants You to Fix the World." It was an extension of a 1999 *Time* cover that featured Federal Reserve chairman Alan Greenspan, with Treasury Secretary Robert Rubin on one side and his successor, Lawrence Summers, on the other, with the words "The Committee to Save the World" in massive type. Think about that trio and their effect on the nation's economy and—especially with Summers—on income inequality, and let that sink in.

And there sat America, waiting to be saved by the celebrity class. Music titans and power couple Jay-Z and Beyoncé surprised one student by paying for his college tuition, writing him a check for $100,000, and continued a tour to surprise ten more. The basketball player Kevin Durant did the same, surprising four of the students he mentored in the Bay Area with a check to pay for their first-year college tuitions.

Then CBS told the heartwarming story of the Alabama public school teacher who struggled to get to work each morning, requiring a labyrinth of public transportation in order to reach class on time. Courtney Adeleye, the CEO of the Mane Choice, a successful hair-care company, discovered that the woman was her daughter's teacher. Adeleye stepped into the breach, put on her cape, and gave the teacher her car. There were tears. There were cameras. The story went international. The morning talk-show circuit soon followed.

In Akron, Ohio, LeBron James opened the I Promise School, an entire public elementary school, paying for its renovation and investing at least $10 million in the school's first years of operation. James agreed to pay for roughly 25 percent of the school's operational costs, while the Akron school district covered the remaining amount. James made a substantial investment, including funding the substitute teachers, paying for the food, and purchasing bicycles and helmets for all 240 students. Two weeks after the I Promise School opened, Alejandro Escude, a Los Angeles poet, wrote a poem titled "LeBron James Will Save the World."

In May 2019, Robert F. Smith, an undergraduate- and graduate-degree Ivy Leaguer, a Goldman Sachs alum, and a venture capitalist billionaire, announced during his Morehouse College commencement address that he would be establishing a $40 million fund to pay off the student loans of the entire graduating class. With his estimated net worth of $5 billion, *Forbes* had recently named Smith the richest black person in America, surpassing Oprah Winfrey. The gift was the largest donation ever to a historically black college or university. The hero game had just gained a new member.

While the celebrities were off saving some people, the rest of the proletariat was left to save itself. The next viral sensation was eleven-year-old Nemiah Martinez of Las Cruces, New Mexico, who opened a lemonade stand to raise money for the kidney and pancreas transplants her mother needed. ABC News ran a piece on this little hero and how she raised $1,100. On the strength of the news report, thousands of dollars more poured in via a GoFundMe account. This was the two-pronged blueprint of the new America: the public had surrendered accountability of its leaders by falling for the gesture and now abdicated responsibility from the state in favor of searching for heroes, whether it was Jay-Z and Beyoncé in their private jet tapping the lucky on the shoulder and paying for their tuition or an adolescent selling lemonade to pay for organ transplants.

THE END OF DAYS

Perhaps the most telling barometer of where we are as a people can be found by the defense of the hero game. Black people especially, I have found, will recoil at the suggestion that there could be anything wrong with Beyoncé paying for college for an at-risk teenager. In 2018, *Forbes* estimated her net worth at $355 million.

Part of the reason is our love of fame and the necessity to protect *black* fame. The athletes and entertainers are the ones who made it. They are our guiding lights, for even though we have, at long last, against long odds, experienced with our own lives the existence of Barack Obama, we also understand just how long those odds were and, quite possibly, how much longer, considering the white reaction that followed, the odds may have become. If history can be considered any type of reliable road map, certain types of successes are even harder to duplicate. "Why," begins an argument I have heard often, "is it wrong that LeBron James wants to do something for the community? Where is the negative in someone using their fame to help others?"

Indeed, there is none, and this is especially true within a framework where, for decades, black athletes were criticized mercilessly for not doing enough for other black people, and one, Michael Jordan, buttressed his on-court iconography with a very (for the 1980s) on-brand campaign of ruthless capitalism as empire. LeBron James, the anti-Jordan in this regard, enjoys a history that is secure and a legacy that will show other inspired athletes that there is strength in helping people. There is nothing wrong with what Robert F. Smith, Kevin Durant, Beyoncé, and Jay-Z are doing. There is nothing wrong with buying a car for a person who educates one's children if that person does not have one. There is nothing inherently wrong with what Bill Gates is doing.

There is, however, everything wrong with what isn't being done around them. As much as it may feel inappropriate to be cynical about an individual building a school in a community that desperately needs one, it is wholly appropriate to critique the phenomenon that surrounds that, for the hero game isn't a cute, celebrity companion to politics where the rich and famous *do their part* by *giving back*. It's a celebrity concierge that is *replacing* politics, replacing infrastructure. The four hundred or so Morehouse students hit the student jackpot, but the following day *USA Today* asked the question, "What about those of us without a billionaire?" The charity of the rich is being treated as an acceptable option to a country that touts itself as the richest in the world, the greatest in the world. It is important to think about what that means: America has reduced itself to a game of celebrity roulette—or industrious elementary schoolers selling lemonade to keep their parents alive.

The deeds of the LeBrons and the Durants and the Oprahs cannot obscure the truth that the hero game exists in a country where half the citizens support a Reagan revolution that has produced the greatest wealth gap in the nation's history, greater even than during the late nineteenth century. The wealth inequality from 1980 to the present has come not only as private wealth explodes but as money for public infrastructure disappears. According to the 2018 *World Inequality Report*, in the postwar years between 1946 and Ronald Reagan's election in 1980, the growth of the national post-tax income was 179 percent for the bottom 20 percent of Americans and 163 percent for the top 0.001 percent. In the years since, between 1980 and 2015, the bottom 20 percent saw its income grow by 4 percent while income for the top 0.001 grew by 616 percent. In dollars, the average salary for an American in the bottom 20 percent of earners was $13,400 in 2014. For their counterparts on the super-rich scale, the number was $90.8 million. As of 2015, the United States possessed the lowest percentage of public wealth (public assets minus debt owed) among wealthy countries— such as Spain, the United Kingdom, France, Germany, and Japan—since 1970, while the American transfer to private wealth over those forty-five years had been astronomical. In 1978, the percentage of American wealth that was public stood at between 10 and 15 percent. Today, when debt is factored into the value of American public assets, the number drops to nearly minus-10 percent, and it is dropping around the Western world. Simultaneously, private wealth, soaring in all industrialized countries, has increased by 500 percent in the US since 1970.

Every January, when the richest people in the world descend on the Swiss Alps hamlet of Davos for the World Economic Forum, the hero game is in full flower. Hundreds of private jets carried the rich world-fixers to the 2019 sessions (including Morehouse savior Robert F. Smith), where the Big Thinkers with the bigger wallets pondered the fate of the world, only to be upstaged by Dutch historian Rutger Bregman, who decided that they were the problem and saw the hero game for precisely the celebrity con it is:

"This is my first time at Davos and I find it quite a bewildering experience to be honest. I mean, 1,500 private jets have flown in here to hear Sir David Attenborough speak about how we're wrecking the planet, and I hear people talking about the language of participation and justice and equality and transparency," he said. "But no one raises the real issue of tax avoidance, of the rich just not paying their fair share. I feel like I'm at a firefighters' conference and no one is allowed to speak about water. . . . Ten years ago, the World Economic Forum asked the question 'What must industry do to prevent broad social backlash?' The answer is very simple: just stop talking about philanthropy and start talking about taxes. Taxes, taxes. . . . This is not rocket science. We can talk a very long time about all these stupid philanthropy schemes. We can invite Bono once more back. We have to be talking about taxes, taxes, taxes. The rest is bullshit, in my opinion."

The hero game cannot be seen without critiquing the massive siphoning off of public money in a nation that should not be grateful that LeBron James built a *public* school as much as it should be insulted that there is apparently no public money to do so; where there is no public infrastructure to keep an eleven-year-old from having to use GoFundMe to pay for treatment for her mother, even though we have the resources for a national healthcare system, just as there is no public infrastructure that would make Beyoncé's and Kevin Durant's gestures welcome instead of necessary. The hero game, whether it is Kim Kardashian positioning herself as a criminal justice savior or Jay-Z handing out scholarships, is not an accident. This country of great wealth is filled with millionaires in government committed to defunding the federal government and avoiding taxes, with the approval of half the voters, and bankrupt in the ways of compassion, shared public space, responsibility, and identity that most make a nation. Maybe instead of giving a teacher a car, we should pay her enough to buy one. None of the celebrity world savers have advocated increasing the public wealth.

At times I wonder if I am misreading our reflexes, and instead of bare-chested exceptionalism, what our friends and neighbors are really expressing through falling for the gesture and their faith in the celebrity safety net is fear, fear that Americans *know* by this stage, whether the topic is the environment, the economy, nuclear geopolitics, or disaster capitalism, that there is no way out. The world's scientists certainly know it. And the reaction is a surrender to it. What we are expressing by making viral videos of hero game examples is not optimism at all but adolescence—a child's need to be taken care of without the possibility of self-determination. We are, in fact, petrified. All of us are a type of Alice Johnson, devoured by a broken system sold to us as thriving, waiting to be rescued, knowing the celebrity lottery is all each of us has left.

THE JOKE'S ON YOU

Periodically and without warning I will ask friends another question: "How do you win at Monopoly?" Given the longevity and ubiquity of the iconic board game, the answer would appear to be so easy that maybe it's a trick question. Though Hasbro (which acquired original owner Parker Brothers in 1991) estimates that a billion people worldwide have played, the objective is not always a given. The most popular answers I receive are usually:

A. To have the most money.
B. To own the most property.
C. To own all the property.
D. When everyone else quits.

The answer, which lies literally within the game's title, is C. The winner is the one who owns *everything*, the player with the monopoly of the board, the one who wipes everyone else out, the one who does capitalism best.

Certain words and phrases find their way into the lexicon, arriving unexpectedly, overstaying like a relative, their departure sometimes a private joy. Post-9/11, *hero* has been peerless for nearly two decades, but *late-stage capitalism* is obnoxiously flapping its arms, desperate to be noticed. It is smug and smarmy, a simultaneously intellectual nod and surrender to our nation-and-planet-destroying ways. It is a wink to cynicism: people positioning themselves as smart enough to recognize the problem while contributing to and profiting from the destruction.

Also, it isn't new. Late-stage capitalism has been present and predicted for more than a century. Certainly, it could have been a phrase Lizzie Magie used in 1902 when she created the Landlord's Game, an anticapitalist response to the Gilded Age pillage of the Carnegies and Mellons, the Dukes, the Schwabs, and the J.P. Morgans. Magie's foreboding board game of runaway wealth at the expense of the people (who faced jail time if, while navigating the treacherous world of rents, utilities, and railroads, they landed on the wrong space) was intended to alarm a society being steamrolled by wealth inequality. In 2011, the magazine *Business Insider* ranked the thirteen richest Americans in history. When adjusted for inflation, ten of the thirteen made their fortunes in Magie's time. The top three—John D. Rockefeller, Andrew Carnegie, and Cornelius Vanderbilt—were not Silicon Valley tech nerds but nineteenth-century robber barons. In 2019, Jeff Bezos, predivorce, was listed by *Forbes* as the richest person in the world with a net worth of $140 billion. At his peak, in today's dollars, Rockefeller was worth *$340 billion*.

Magie's game acquired many nicknames, and one, "the Monopoly Game," gained traction. Players soon took to simply calling it "Monopoly," and it stuck, eventually becoming the inspiration for Charles Darrow's 1935 version that he sold to Massachusetts game maker Parker Brothers during the height of the Great Depression. In the decades that followed, the signal ostensibly alerting Americans to the perils of a winner-take-all society would become their signature badge of honor, the most famous board game this country has ever produced, a societal aspiration instead of an orthodoxy to be rejected.

OPEN SEASON

No financial sector has more money at its disposal than the federal government, and with the lure of trillions of taxpayer dollars and the opportunity to weaken the government as an adversary, the billionaire class couldn't resist the temptation to invade politics. Donald Trump (net worth $3.1 billion in 2019) ushered in the first billionaire presidency with a billionaire cabinet (*Forbes* estimated the combined net worth of Trump's inaugural cabinet to be $4.6 billion) packaged around the political ideology of reducing "government waste." Its true aim, however, was completing what Ronald Reagan had started: eliminating the social responsibilities of the federal government to the people—but not before stealing taxpayer money in ways even Reagan never imagined. "I want people," Trump said in response to criticism of his billionaire public servants who would serve only themselves, "who have made a fortune." The assault strategy to reduce regulation, neuter oversight agencies, and privatize public programs that further extended private wealth while weakening the public was brazenly unhidden. Whatever was left of the government would then be used to feed the American oligarchy, shifting public money to private wealth.

"The president and his aides," the *New York Times* reported in October 2018, "have repeatedly shown they are willing to use the government's prestige and power to help their friends and relatives make money." While the rank-and-file Americans, the Fox Newsers, and the MSNBCers, duke out their ideologies over Thanksgiving dinner, the billionaires have taken over the Monopoly board—and the board is America.

Scott Pruitt, Donald Trump's first head of the Environmental Protection Agency (EPA), joined Washington with a net worth of $3.2 million. Despite being a millionaire, he wasn't a billionaire, and thus Pruitt was somewhat lampooned in media circles as the poor kid of the administration. He knew the billionaire playbook, though, and used the EPA as his personal expense account, using thousands of taxpayer dollars to travel first class and for his security detail—even taking his taxpayer-funded bodyguards to Disneyland. He argued that traveling first class was necessary because in America's toxic political climate, being seated with coach passengers endangered his safety. He spent the public's money to use military planes in nonmilitary zones.

Pruitt used his influence as the head of a government agency for personal advancement—a clear conflict of interest—to inquire about acquiring a franchise license in a fast-food chain for his wife, as well as the spoils of the gilded for himself, when he accepted tickets to the 2018 Rose Bowl to watch his beloved Oklahoma Sooners—from an agency that represents oil and gas companies, the very industry over which Pruitt was supposed to have oversight.

Bloomberg and ABC News reported that Pruitt lived in a condominium owned by a lobbyist whose husband lobbied the EPA, and Pruitt was accused by congressional members and watchdog agencies of purposely circumventing public record-keeping procedures. Meanwhile, while Pruitt's skimming from a numb public garnered the headlines, his real purpose was to weaken the EPA. Before taking over the agency he argued for its abolition. He spent his time in office rolling back Obama-era landmark climate-change regulations so corporations wouldn't have to worry about the EPA getting in their way if, say, they wanted to mine in the Arctic. "Over the past 13 months," the *Guardian* reported, "Pruitt's EPA has taken at least 15 major actions on air pollution—all to delay, weaken or repeal protections, and all opposed by the American Lung Association and other health groups—according to an analysis by the office of Sen. Jeff Merkley (D-Ore.)."

In other words, Pruitt followed the script to perfection. He used his position to declaw EPA oversight of corporate polluters and use taxpayer money to fly first class. Pruitt lasted eighteen months before resigning, devoured by several ethics probes.

Panic, a 2018 VICE News/HBO documentary on the 2008 financial crisis, posited the theory that Trump's rise was due to populist anger over the Obama administration not being tough enough on the dubious actors who ran the global economy into ruin. Not only did none of those people go to prison under Obama, but Wall Street influence in government only increased with Trump. Pundits even had a nickname for the money train steamrolling the government. With alums Steve Mnuchin (net worth $300 million) in charge of Treasury, Gary Cohn (assets ranging from $252 million to dividends that push that number to $611 million) at the National Economic Council, and Jay Clayton ($50 million) at the Securities and Exchange Commission continuing the tradition of Wall Street insiders taking Washington jobs to police their insider friends, Goldman Sachs is commonly and derisively known as "Government Sachs." As Inequality.org wrote of the cozy relationship, "Trump has turned to Wall Street veterans with deep knowledge of the financial crisis—knowledge gained as champions of the dangerous practices that helped cause it."

Following Trump, his gilded cabinet went about the business of profiting from the presidency without consequence. Like Pruitt, Mnuchin tried to use military planes—paid for by taxpayers—for private trips, once unsuccessfully requesting a government plane to take his wife on a European honeymoon. In 2017 alone he spent upward of $800,000 of public money on personal travel. No one is even attempting to hide the grift. Bill Foley, owner of the NHL's Vegas Golden Knights, contributed to Ryan Zinke's congressional campaign and to Trump's inauguration. Trump appointed Zinke secretary of the Interior, and Zinke proceeded to give a twelve-minute speech to the hockey team. Using government money, Zinke chartered a flight from Las Vegas to Montana—for $12,000.

In a 2017 social media response to being called "deplorable" after captioning a photo of herself deplaning with hashtags of the designer fashions she was wearing, Mnuchin's wife, Louise Linton, explained what is occurring unambiguously: these are the spoils of being rich. "Have you ever given more to the economy than me and my husband?" she posted in a gauche online clapback. During the thirty-five-day government shutdown from December 2018 to January 2019, Secretary of Commerce Wilbur Ross (net worth $700 million) said he didn't "really quite understand" why furloughed workers had been visiting homeless shelters and food pantries in lieu of receiving their paychecks. This is the same Ross who was confirmed by the Senate 72–27, even while being sued by a former equity partner for stealing millions of dollars of his share of a private equity fund, one of many allegations against Ross. "All told, these allegations—which sparked, lawsuits, reimbursements and an SEC fine—come to more than $120 million," *Forbes* wrote of Ross in summer 2018. "If even half of the accusations are legitimate, the current United States secretary of commerce could rank among the biggest grifters in American history."

In April 2019, Public Citizen released an "update on the corporate takeover of our government: An oil lobbyist runs the DOI. A coal lobbyist runs the EPA. A pharma exec runs HHS. A Boeing exec runs DOD. A billionaire Amway heiress runs DoED. A private equity kingpin runs Commerce. A Goldman Sachs exec runs Treasury."

The update needed updating. The national disgrace of migrant detention centers at the southern border was defining not only of the administration that revels in the inhumanity of its policies but also of Americans, who treated the death, sexual abuse, and misconducts that occurred within the camps with a callousness that mirrored the president. Cruelty for profit is America's business card, confirmed by the subsequent departure of White House chief of staff General John Kelly. Kelly, often referred to by a desperate, normalizing press corps as "the adult in the room," left the Trump White House in 2018 and the next year joined the board of Caliburn International, which runs the largest detention facility for unaccompanied migrant children, based in Homestead, Florida. This is who we are.

The Trump cabinet saw opportunity and arrived in Washington with one mission: to defund and defang the federal government for the benefit of the corporate state. It bet that *democracy, freedom, justice,* words Americans cling to without demanding accounting to their meaning, didn't need to be overcome. They would simply show up and take. The public wouldn't even fight for their cherished bedrocks. They're too busy ripping each other to shreds.

The 2018 *World Inequality Report* is a truly devastating document, and while the public money disappears the public infrastructure people take for granted is systematically being snatched away. Hailed as a model for successful public-private partnership, New York City's Bryant Park is supported by the Rockefeller Fund and has been run by a private management firm since 1988, which is great when tourists want to ice skate in between Christmas shopping, but not so much when security can shut down a public rally because the park that has belonged to the public since 1686 is no longer technically public. While Zinke is charging taxpayers $12,000 to fly from Las Vegas to Montana, he advocates privatizing America's national parks, aided by Trump cutting the 2017 funding for the National Park Service by $400 million. Americans, both in the Congress they have elected and their spiritless response to the naked grifting by its public servants, have given them a license to maraud. The store is open.

The corruption of the American dream has created the pillaging, and the disinterested public response to it. Owning one's home and ensuring that the child enjoyed better opportunities than the parents—if the dream was ever truly that—has given way to the conviction that through whiteness, ruthlessness, and an utter amorality, one day they could become tomorrow's conquerors and walk away with an obscene pile of money. They could brag about the latest flip, the perfectly legal swindle America has mastered the art of preemptively excusing itself.

PROFILES IN COWARDICE

"Conflicts are just the trade-off for picking an SEC chair with deep industry knowledge and experience," the legal newsletter *Above the Law* wrote about Jay Clayton. During baseball's infamous steroid era, the counter to any suggestion that there should be integrity during a cynical time was *Well, you would have taken the money too*, followed by "If you ain't cheating, you ain't trying." In order to confront the joke being on us we break bad in methods large and small to cash in as well. All of which contributes to the way, way down. Whether it's Rupert Murdoch's Fox News or NBC, the conservative-leaning Sinclair Broadcast Group or CNN, the heads of broadcast networks contributing to political candidates or parties has led to political journalists endorsing candidates they cover. Sports networks being business partners with the leagues whose games they broadcast has produced journalists who make deals with the production companies of professional athletes, whose millions have made them power players in the media space. It creates journalists who are not journalists at all. Somehow, these reporters believe that their word of honor alone exempts them from their participation in this enormous and obvious con. As the money flows beyond comprehension, many reporters cashing in have said that entering journalism did not mean taking an oath of poverty. But being a journalist means exactly that, sacrificing financially, if the money you could earn is going to be extracted from the people and institutions you are charged with holding accountable. It is a glib, self-forgiving, and self-deluding position, a justification for them taking their slice. We condone their behavior because it allows us to excuse our own.

Business executives slide effortlessly between the public and private sectors, each so thoroughly compromised that consumer protection seems a quaint concept. Whether it's Hank Paulson, Lawrence Summers, or any one of the endless roster of suits who enter *public service*, a consequence is the normalizing of conflicts of interest, to the point where being compromised is not treated as unethical and a threat to our institutions but as essential. In sports, at least on the broadcast side, reporters have been largely replaced by ex-athletes and ex-coaches who use their fame and position to blur and eliminate the lines of conflict, normalizing conflicts and cashing in. In team sports, television networks allow fired coaches to use the broadcast booth as a way station, a daily audition for their next job. In tennis, broadcasters comment on a pool of players and tournaments for whom they may one day be working. The former player James Blake works for Tennis Channel but is also the tournament director of the Miami Open. Tennis Channel has in its stable Lindsay Davenport, Paul Annacone, and Jim Courier. Davenport was the coach of Madison Keys, Annacone of Alex de Minaur (and before that Sloane Stephens and Roger Federer). While broadcasting his opinions, Courier, meanwhile, was the coach of the US Davis Cup team. Justin Gimelstob coached John Isner, and Martina Navratilova briefly coached Agnieszka Radwanska.

At ESPN, Darren Cahill served as coach of Simona Halep, John McEnroe coached Milos Raonic, and McEnroe's brother Patrick was both coach of the US Davis Cup (preceding Courier) and president of the US Tennis Association (USTA). While serving in the broadcast booth, Patrick Mouratoglou coached Serena Williams, Stefanos Tsitsipas, and Coco Gauff. Rennae Stubbs served as a broadcaster and also the coach of Karolina Pliskova. Mary Jo Fernandez was the coach of the US Federation Cup team, and her husband is business partners with Roger Federer. In a toothless nod to professionalism, often a broadcaster/coach refrains from calling the matches of one of his or her players, but it is hardly a prohibition of value, for they are still commenting on other players, including their own pre- and postmatch, any of whom may one day become future clients. Additionally, with the airwaves cluttered by people in business, critical analysis of the tennis industry is virtually nonexistent. For example, Gimelstob, the players' representative to the Association of Tennis Professionals (ATP) board, pleaded no contest to a felony battery charge, and no network covered a word of it. Gimelstob's conflicts ran so deep (his production company was also a partner with the USTA), that he brazenly planned to run to head the ATP, giving an embarrassingly entitled interview to the *New York Times* in which he said he simply outworked his contemporaries. Only the pressure from fellow players and social media forced Gimelstob to back away and resign, from both the ATP and Tennis Channel. He was never sanctioned by any of the sport's governing bodies. Only public pressure forced his hand. This club is so cozy all it needs is a fireplace.

Whether it is in team sports or the political airwaves being composed of party operatives, a free press is being killed without a shot being fired. Considering the naked and very public looting of the federal government, it is no surprise that the conflicts in something as ostensibly ephemeral as sports get a pass. Everyone is doing it.

THE ROYAL LOOTERS

On May 11, 2017, I received an email from my credit card company alerting me to the fantastic news: my credit limit was being raised by several thousand dollars. I called immediately. I did not request a credit line increase and was wary of potentially using more credit just because I had more. If being such a good customer was going to produce preferential treatment, I might as well ask for something I actually wanted: a lower interest rate.

The perky young lady on the phone could not have been friendlier in denying my request for a lower APR. The 20-plus-percent interest rate, despite my good standing, she said, was "standard." I asked if there was an airline card with a lower interest rate to which I could transfer my balance. The answer was no. Even with an excellent-to-perfect credit score, I was told, most credit cards, especially cards for airline miles rewards, adhered to an annual interest rate of 20 to 24 percent.

What, then, I asked, was the real value of maintaining

excellent credit if the percentage of interest I was paying never decreased?

"Well," she said enthusiastically, "you'll qualify for faster and larger credit increases, and a higher credit limit reduces your credit utilization and you'll be more likely to be approved for our most prestigious cards."

During this same period, the same credit card company, without alerting me, rewarded my financial diligence not only by raising my credit limit but also by surreptitiously raising the interest rate of the card. For being a good customer with excellent credit, my reward was not to pay less interest on money I had proven I would pay back responsibly, but to be able to go deeper into debt, borrowing more money at a higher interest rate.

"Surreptitious" was the appropriate word, for the only way I discovered any of this was occurring was when a letter arrived from my credit card company sixteen months later, stating the following:

Dear Howard Bryant,

Every six months, we review accounts that previously had an Annual Percentage Rate (APR) increase to determine if the APR should be reduced. These semi-annual reviews are a requirement of Regulation Z under the Credit Card Accountability, Responsibility and Disclosure (CARD) Act. Due to flaws in our methodology, we are issuing you a refund for excess interest previously charged to your account.

Attached is a refund check for $273.03. . . . This refund check is being issued in accordance with an agreement between (MY BANK) and the Bureau of Consumer Financial Protection. Under the agreement, (MY BANK) is providing refunds to customers who, between February 2011 and February 2018, incurred higher interest charges due to flaws in our semi-annual APR review methodology.

In May 2009, five months after taking office, Barack Obama signed the CARD Act into law. Nine months later, CARD went into effect. Its aim was to produce transparency, to provide the consumer with some knowledge of the fees and interest rates credit card companies were charging, as well as make it easier for people with poor credit to improve their credit and not be subject to predatory lending practices. The law also eliminated the tawdry practice of targeting minors and college students with credit card offers, an exploitation of vulnerable college kids popularized during Reagan's deregulated 1980s. The bill, broadly supported by both parties, passed overwhelmingly and was celebrated as a victory for the average person getting whacked by high interest rates and vulturelike behavior from credit card companies.

What, in real time, was actually happening to the real person? The real person, if he or she is black, is drowning. In 2015 the Federal Reserve Bank of Boston, in partnership with Duke University and the New School, released a stunning report titled *The Color of Wealth in Boston*, which studied wealth inequality in the city and sounded the nuclear alarm. "The net worth of whites as compared with nonwhites is staggeringly divergent," the study found.

White households in the Boston area had a median net worth of $247,500. The net worth of American-born blacks was *eight dollars*. The gap in average value of liquid assets (checking and savings accounts, money-market accounts, stocks, or government bonds that could be turned into cash) was enormous: $25,000 for white households, $670 for US black ones. "For every dollar the typical white household has in liquid assets (excluding cash), US blacks have two cents," the study reported. "Caribbean blacks have 14 cents and Puerto Ricans and Dominicans less than one cent." The study noted that close to half of Puerto Ricans and a quarter of US blacks qualified as "unbanked," which was to say they did not have a checking or savings account, yet 52.3 percent of US blacks reported having credit card debt, compared to 46.5 percent of white households. "Unless net worth outcomes in communities of color improve, the aggregate magnitude of the wealth disparity will increase," the study concluded. "This is a first-order public policy problem requiring immediate attention."

Yet there were the credit card companies, offering up more debt at higher interest rates, in tandem with credit agencies whose algorithms make it easier for poor people to qualify for debt that hurts them (credit cards) and harder for debt that leads to equity (housing loans). But their representatives had excellent phone manners.

While the Consumer Financial Protection Bureau (CFPB) was barely doing its job keeping watch on massive financial corporations, the Trump administration continued its assault on the public, requesting a second-quarter CFPB budget in 2018 of . . . drumroll . . . $0.00, which would exhaust the revenues of the department, making it virtually impossible for the CFPB to investigate industries—whether it be those issuing student loans or the consumer credit market—preying on consumers. *Forbes* described the Trump administration's action as "killing the Consumer Protection Agency by a thousand cuts." In May 2018 the *Chicago Tribune* reported that the student lending office of the CFPB had returned $750 million in relief to consumers affected by the abuses in the student loan market, a $1.5 trillion industry. Mick Mulvaney, then Trump's CFPB head, responded by closing the bureau's student lending office. Mulvaney's successor, Kathy Kraninger, continued the assault, announcing in 2019 her intention to undo a 2015 Obama-era rule that provided transparency in bank lending.

The attacks on the function of government are coordinated and deliberate. While America remained distracted by tweets, the Federal Elections Commission, watchdog of campaign violations, fraud, and how money is spent, not dissimilar to the CFPB, disclosed in August 2019 that it was shutting down due to a lack of members for quorum. After the 2016 campaign was affected by foreign interference and misinformation, the 2020 campaign began with no oversight agency. This is what they want.

Meanwhile, Education Secretary Betsy DeVos (net worth $1.25 billion), wife of Dick DeVos of Amway and the Orlando Magic, is doing her part to dismantle public education. Like Pruitt and Mulvaney, DeVos serves two purposes for the Trump administration: to bleed dry what existing dollars remain in the public education system in favor of privatization and to do away with federal rules protecting the civil rights of students. In her home state of Michigan, one of the worst sexual abuse scandals in the country's history occurred at USA Gymnastics, whose head doctor, Michigan State University physician Larry Nassar, was convicted of sexually abusing at least 250 female gymnasts, many of whom were minors at the time, including some of the most celebrated names in the sport. Nassar was sentenced to more than sixty years in prison. Michigan State University president Lou Anna Simon resigned, as did the athletic director, Mark Hollis. The university agreed to pay out upward of $500 million in settlements to more than three hundred victims.

Concurrently, DeVos had been working to reduce protections for victims of sexual assault at colleges and universities that receive federal funding and make it harder for schools to be held accountable for their child abusers, their Jerry Sanduskys and Larry Nassars. DeVos also rescinded two Obama-era Title IX guidelines, including assault protections for transgender students.

The largely discredited for-profit college industry is already in debt to DeVos, for one of her first orders of business after being appointed by Trump was to close investigations begun under the Obama administration into for-profit colleges that defrauded students financially and provided them with worthless degrees.

No Is Not Enough, the Canadian journalist Naomi Klein's 2017 forensic takedown of the Trump kleptocracy and the politico-corporate strategy of profiting from global disruption, begins with a quote. It is from the late Native American activist and poet John Trudell. "I'm not looking to overthrow the American government," he said. "The corporate state already has."

The store, indeed, is open. Without much resistance from government investigators and regulators, corporations run wild in ways catastrophic (the 2008 global financial crisis) and small. The credit-reporting industry faced no sanction or reform for the 2017 Equifax data breach that exposed the personal financial data of some 143 million Americans, according to the Federal Trade Commission, and the diligent consumers who practice good credit habits might be disturbed to know that the three major reporting agencies—Equifax, TransUnion, and Experian—use different rating models depending on the type of consumer loan. The most consumer-friendly credit scores are for credit cards, the most punitive for mortgages. The joke, perhaps unclear at first, is on the consumer: it's easier for a person to get a credit card (credit that only increases debt) than for the same person to obtain a mortgage (credit that increases personal wealth).

Take, also, for example the innovation the Marriott Corporation was given credit for: around the same time Trump began defunding the CFPB, the hotel giant, in 2017, began charging a $25-per-day "destination fee" for designated New York hotels. Marriott already charged a "resort fee" for upkeep of its properties in vacation paradises such as the Caribbean or other all-inclusive locales. It referred to the charge as a "pilot program," which was corporate-speak for checking to see if they could get away with it. They did. Hilton and Hyatt immediately followed. Rightfully, consumer advocates called the $25-per-day charge a "hidden fee," but the CFPB never investigated. It was likely too busy trying to avoid Trump's guillotine and stay in business. On January 1, 2019, the looting continued. The Grand Hyatt New York, which just happens to be the hotel Donald Trump renovated to begin his ascent in New York real estate forty years ago, increased its "destination fee" to $30 per day. Beginning

December 1, 2018, two Hyatts in Boston and three in San Francisco began charging guests a "destination fee" of $22.89 for the right to check in. One real estate executive mentioned a "surprising lack of public outrage" as a reason the pilot program became standard so quickly. Nobody tried to stop them, so the hotels took what they wanted. They are running unopposed.

A handful, a snatch, a glimpse of all the puzzle pieces shows how the joke's on you. Undermined by grift large and small, Americans react with a smile, like the boxer who takes a straight right to the face. It is a punishing blow, one he can feel in his knees and his heart, the pain shattering both his brain and resolve. He smiles, lying to himself and his opponent with a face that says, *That didn't hurt. You cannot hurt me.* Soon he is on the mat, looking up, being counted out.

The puzzle pieces interlock. The gruesome picture forms. The public uses phrases like *late-stage capitalism*, the equivalent of the boxer's smile, its way of saying, *I get it. I'm ahead of you*, when they are actually despairing, saying, *There's nothing I can do.* They think they get it when they are really closer to getting knocked out.

How does "getting it" manifest in a world of unaccountable multinational corporations, corporate-controlled journalism, a deregulated, looted government, and a Supreme Court that supports them? Oftentimes the stated formula is building a sufficient retirement fund to serve as a firewall before the devouring, combined with what people—who have the resources to actually save for retirement—refer to as "conscientious investing." In my city, people are obsessed with living not only healthily but conscientiously, with farm-to-table food, farm shares, farmers' markets, and fair-trade commerce, as well as protests against police brutality and mass incarceration and in favor of gender and transgender equality and clean energy. Gas-guzzling cars are ridiculed. At least half of the weeks of the year a public protest occurs somewhere in town. This Massachusetts town is, or likes to think of itself as, a do-gooders' paradise.

Yet nestled into the mutual funds of their 401(k)s are companies like CCA, the Corrections Corporation of America. It is the second-largest for-profit prison firm in the nation and its stock can be found throughout the retirement portfolios of Vanguard and Fidelity, the two largest retirement-management companies in America. It may have changed its name to the friendlier-sounding CoreCivic but it is still CCA, a prime engine (or at least major benefactor) of locking up people—mostly black people—for money. The people who plant "No Pipeline" signs on their front lawns or the more committed who trudged out in the rain to protest the Keystone pipeline or made the pilgrimage to South Dakota in solidarity with the 2016 Standing Rock protests very likely are funding their retirements with the energy stocks bundled in mutual funds to build their 401(k) firewall against late-stage capitalism.

"Look at Apple. They manufacture in China, so you're probably dealing with some form of cheap labor/sweatshop element. You can be conscientious, and there are portfolios that focus on being socially aware, and now you can invest without significant loss of returns," a Massachusetts financial planner told me. "Look at energy. Even if you invest in solar, solar panels have to get made somewhere, and it's probably not here. They're being made somewhere with the cheapest labor costs. And as you build, how much are you sacrificing returns? There is definitely a disconnect."

CASH RULES

In a just world, the legacy of Lizzie Magie and the Landlord's Game would be an alarm about the destructiveness of unchecked capitalism heeded by an engaged people embittered by inequality and wary of the influence of money on a democracy, but justice has never been much of a match for money. A widow with no children, Magie died in 1948, her contribution to the country's most famous board game largely unknown, and the game she patented in 1904 became exactly the opposite of her intention. Monopoly only produced more capitalism, the glorification of it, the celebration of it. There have been more than 1,100 different commercialized limited-edition brand themes of the classic game, from *Game of Thrones* Monopoly and Harry Potter Monopoly, to Boston Red Sox Monopoly, *Fortnite* Monopoly, and *Mario Kart* Monopoly. There is even—in the perhaps the greatest nod to the American empire—McDonald's Monopoly.

In a world of Mnuchins and Pruitts, Trumps and PEDs, Hasbro unironically introduced Monopoly, Cheaters Edition. The sales tag line for the game was changed from the original "The Property Trading Game from Parker Brothers" to "What Can *You* Get Away With?" In this version, players are allowed to steal from the bank and from each other. "The rules encourage players to express their inner cheater to own it all while they buy, sell, dream and scheme. . . . Players can try to get away with as many cheats as they can. . . . Ages 8 and up." There are no houses in this game—perhaps houses are not ambitious enough—but only hotels. The game even comes with plastic handcuffs, a hollow fidelity to the idea that white-collar theft still brings consequences, but the handcuffs might be the only false note in the game. Cheaters don't go to jail these days. They become president. Perhaps it is all ironic, for Monopoly: Cheaters Edition was released June 1, 2018, eighteen months into the Trump kleptocracy. Maybe, but do not count on it. There is nothing cautionary about this version. Maybe, by never living to see this catastrophe, Lizzie Magie had the last laugh after all.

POSTSCRIPT

RENTERS

The dream of America can be found on television. Shiny, new-car-smell consumerism, golden-brown French fries in slow-motion free-falling across the flat screen just a commercial away. The reality of America is at the airport, with its runaway obesity; gooey, shitty food; and gluttonous, duty-free excess. The dream is marketable. The reality is not.

The airport is America's modern-day Manassas, the ugly battleground where the nation, through public sloganeering, bares its teeth: the red versus the blue, the black and the white, the outnumbered protesters and the faux patriots. Since the beginning of the Obama years, when postracialism became pre-apocalypse, Americans have been ratcheting up the hyperbole. The punditry talks of "a second civil war." Can we all get along? No.

Through the act of getting dressed, Americans have committed to fighting one another. As they board their flights, these human bumper stickers wage their cold civil war, weaponizing and defending their positions on beer bellies across the country. In Atlanta, a white man wears a T-shirt that reads "I Stand for the Flag . . . and Kneel for the Cross," an obvious response to Colin Kaepernick and the black athletes who have the nerve to believe Chicago police needn't have shot Laquan McDonald sixteen times. Twenty feet from him another man, a black man, enters the jet bridge for his connection to Little Rock wearing a black T-shirt with the familiar logo of the National Football League centered on his chest, but instead of the letters "NFL" emblazoned in red across the shield, the letters "KAP" replace them, a raised fist on the logo replacing the football. I'm on the Little Rock flight, and as the passengers board, the scene of a million trips to the airport in post-9/11 America repeats itself: a significant volume of sports clothing underscores the militarized nationalism—the American flag on shirts, camouflage yoga pants, baseball caps representing a branch of the military—that has devoured the country since the towers fell. Ten days later, I watch a barrel-chested man board a flight to New Orleans, his pale-green shirt shouting at me "MY SON HAS YOUR BACK. PROUD ARMY DAD," the words superimposed over an American flag. In Hartford, Connecticut, an older white man walks the terminal advertising America's imperial depravity as patriotism, reducing the two bloodiest conflicts in human history to a grotesque buzzer-beater, another championship trophy to be raised by the Greatest Nation in the World. The shirt is black with an American flag filling the geographical shape of the United States in the center, bordered to the north and south by the words "BACK TO BACK: WORLD WAR CHAMPS." If there is a score to be kept, it is of the 40 million worldwide deaths in World War I and the 85 million deaths—an estimated 3 percent of the earth's human population at the time—in World War II. The nationalism is infused not with a love of country but a menacing whiteness, a weaponizing of symbols of power, identity, and words —a reminder of to whom this country really belongs. The reminder is not directed at a foreign power but to the nonwhites in America. It is most certainly a reclaiming.

For a dozen years now, their fear has been pointing, spitting, and snarling, on the congressional floor (see: Joe Wilson's "You lie!" to President Obama), on television, and at the ballot box. Now, it snarls through their clothing. The American flag has been reclaimed and in many ways restored from a lofty, aspirational ideal to cold representation of its present reality, no more visionary welcome banner but threat. The flag is celebrated even when it is desecrated—when commercialized by stars-and-stripes Speedos and bikinis or in the name of the police, when it is altered from the red, white, and blue into the authoritarian black, white, and blue allegiance to a single constituency: police and their sympathizers. *Blue Lives Matter*, a response not to the difficulty of police work but to the audacity of citizens, especially the black ones, daring to challenge cops. Had its existence been dedicated to the former, Blue Lives Matter wouldn't have required black protest as its incubator. It would have predated Michael Brown.

America's obsession with war, its obsession with cops, the passive-aggressive messaging from citizens, the illegal militias at the border, and the cop-calling white women are a reinforcement of whiteness. War is an authoritarian response to the black and brown internationally, blind fealty to police another to the kneelers and dissenters, the black and brown at home. The T-shirts and hats are again marking territory. A black friend is convinced that a cornered whiteness is the most dangerous whiteness, and though whites are willing to ignore the data of global warming they are certainly unwilling to dismiss the data that America will soon become a majority-minority country. That, they believe. No matter how many white men still overwhelm the Fortune 500 list, no matter how many mediocre white boys dominate the rank and file of corporate America, much of the white race acts as if they are under a Code Red threat. Their America is being taken from them. The information on the stuff they buy is still in English—but it's in Spanish too.

This friend believes the whites will respond to feeling under threat by eventually taking its country back by force, that Charlottesville was an amuse-bouche and whites have decided to not go down without a fight, that the cold civil war of T-shirts and mean tweets will turn hot, to AR-15s and bloodshed. He, too, does not reject data—the data indicating that, encouraged by Donald Trump, white supremacist groups are regaining strength across the country. Anyone who has done even a cursory amount of research on the subject knows my friend is not exaggerating. Nor does he reject the data showing that hundreds of former and active police and military are part of white nationalist, antigovernment groups. In response, he has joined a "social group" of like-minded African American men. They frequent the shooting range. He obtained his concealed-weapons permit. "They're not getting me without me taking some of them with me," he tells me.

Then and now, whether a T-shirt or an oversize American (sometimes joined by Confederate) flag bolted to the beds of a pickup truck, the message is the same: to be nonwhite is to be a renter of the American dream. It is to be reminded that one's citizenship is always tenuous and that one's white neighbors, who consider themselves the owners, think it can be summarily revoked, sometimes legally but always emotionally, anecdotally, figuratively. This is the root of the culture war being fought on the campaign trail and in airport terminals across America. The nonwhite presence in America, regardless of claim or service, years distant from Appomattox or Selma, is always reminded that the white public believes it is, and will always be, more American than you.

GO BACK TO AFRICA

Being treated as a renter is a certainty of being black in the United States, yet most white Americans grow red with indignation at the suggestion that white supremacy exists. They do this while spending much of their time ensuring its stability, either through the magic of *not seeing color* or the fierce, ahistorical insistence that black people actually have it *better* than whites. "The trigger for white rage, inevitably, is black advancement," Carol Anderson wrote in her book *White Rage*. "It is not the mere presence of black people that is the problem; rather, it is blackness with ambition, with drive, with purpose, with aspirations, and with demands for full and equal citizenship."[1] It was full citizenship—meaning the ability to demand accountability from law enforcement—that black athletes expressed through protest, and it was denial of that citizenship when the president of the United States said of the athletes, "Maybe they don't belong in this country." (This is the office that people such as Tiger Woods said should always be respected.) There was nothing ahistorical about the president's response. When I was a columnist for the *Boston Herald*, I nicknamed my hate mail folder the "Back to Africa File" because invariably disagreeing with my positions about the Red Sox or Patriots wasn't enough. Nor was calling me a faggot, a pussy, or a nigger. What was crucial for so many white readers offended by my column about last Tuesday night's Red Sox–Angels game was their belief that I was borrowing something that not only wasn't mine but that specifically belonged to them, and as such they could take it away.

The reflex to figuratively deport a fellow citizen through the ease of language—*Go back to Africa*—is one of the easiest tells of a white supremacy we're so often told does not exist. *Maybe they don't belong in the country.* The threat to remove another individual *who is already home* is a rare and special entitlement. It borders, even, on the preposterous. Unless, of course, you're not home. Unless, of course, the person sending you away not only believes that you are not home but is secure in the belief that they are.

During the first Democratic presidential debate, something darkened in me as I listened to Kamala Harris spar with Joe Biden over his position on school desegregation in the 1970s. "I appreciate all you've done for our country," she said. *Our* country. She said it easily, and confidently, a secure claiming of the space as assuredly as calling a house one has purchased "my house." Certainly, we have paid, overpaid and dearly, for this piece of land—with money and blood. Yet when I heard the words, *whenever* I hear the words, they sound clever and earnest and wholly unconvincing, because they collide so meekly and inauthentically with our daily bludgeoning. I listened to

Harris and felt the same despair I felt eleven years earlier listening to Barack Obama expose himself, both for his own ego and ambition, but also for us. Not three weeks after Harris's comments, Donald Trump, criticized for his inhuman border policies by Congresswomen Ayanna Pressley, Rashida Tlaib, Ilhan Omar, and Alexandria Ocasio-Cortez, reminded them, elected members of the House of Representatives, that they, too, were just renters. "Go back and fix the totally broken and crime-infested places from which they came," he tweeted. Democrats denounced the comments but didn't exactly put their legs into it. Not a single Republican condemned him. They are thinking just as he does, as so many of their constituents do.

Saying *our* in the presence of white people is taken by them as support for *their* country, not ownership of one's own. It is to say, "You, white people, are in charge, and we support you." That is how they interpret the black relationship to *our*. When black people use *our* in the presence of other black people, white people do not view it as brotherhood or as countrymen, but as a threat. They hear a takeover. We want it to be ours. We know it to be ours. We bled for it to be ours. We also know that it is not.

None of this, it should be noted, is new, and the venerability of the question is precisely why so many whites feel so comfortable, even at this ostensibly postracial (post-postracial?) date, opining on the validity of black citizenship while never questioning their own. The daily, extralegal threats of being kidnapped into slavery were a scourge for all free blacks, criminal acts reinforced by the moral and legal authority of the US Supreme Court, which ruled in the 1857 *Dred Scott* case that no African American under any circumstance could be deemed a citizen of the United States. "On the eve of the Civil War nearly half a million people, the majority of them born in the United States, lived with their rights always subject to the threat of removal," Martha S. Jones wrote in her book *Birthright Citizens*. In 2018 and 2019, as immigration raids and lethal, children-killing border camps defined America's attitudes, the Supreme Court prepared to hear arguments on cases regarding birthright citizenship, more than 150 years after the adoption of the Thirteenth and Fourteenth amendments. Renters live under the threat of eviction. Owners cannot be evicted.

NOT YOUR MASCOT

Rob Manfred, the commissioner of Major League Baseball, has degrees from Cornell University and Harvard Law School. The general manager layer of baseball management boasts the Ivy League elite, the very best minds from the very best universities this country has to offer. During 2018 and moving into the 2019 baseball season, America's educational elites were well represented: there were Sandy Alderson (Dartmouth, Harvard Law), Mark Shapiro (Princeton), Rick Hahn (Harvard Law), Jeff Bridich (Harvard), Theo Epstein (Yale), Mike Elias (Yale), Jon Daniels (Cornell), David Forst (Harvard), A. J. Preller (Cornell), Mike Hazen (Princeton), Matt Klentak (Dartmouth), David Stearns (Harvard), Matt Silverman (Harvard), and Jeff Luhnow (Penn). Among the non-Ivies, there's no drop-off in pedigree with Farhan Zaidi (MIT), Thad Levine (Haverford), Jed Hoyer (Amherst), Derek Falvey (Trinity), and Chris Antonetti (Georgetown).

With such formidable credentials among its ranks, the culture of the sport coopted by the super-elites, one would think a GM would be able to end poverty *and* make a blockbuster deal, all before the trade deadline. Instead, despite all those tuition dollars and endowments and legacy, baseball apparently needs to be told right from wrong, like kindergartners who have to be told not to call other kids names. It did, unintentionally, offer the country a master class in power, owners versus renters.

One ubiquitous image ran throughout the epic 2016 World Series between the Chicago Cubs and Cleveland Indians, and it wasn't of delirious Cubs fans sloshing beer on one another after their eventual champions scored yet another run. It was the red face of Chief Wahoo, the Cleveland mascot, as racist and demeaning as ever, emblazoned on the sleeves of the Indians' uniforms and on the front of their baseball caps, the caricature of big teeth and the dishonest smile preceding deception.

Manfred would say, completely unconvincingly, that there is no place for racism in the game of baseball. He was wrong, of course. There is absolutely a place for racism in baseball, and that place is on the jerseys and in the team stores of Cleveland's and Atlanta's baseball clubs, on the blankets, the T-shirts, and the foam fingers they sell. There is a place for racism in baseball, with the Indians and with the tomahawk-chopping Atlanta Braves, just as there is in hockey with the Chicago Blackhawks, in pro football with the Washington Redskins, and in college football with the Florida State Seminoles.

During a press conference before Game 2 of that World Series, sitting next to Henry Aaron and David Ortiz, Manfred did the worst thing a white man in his position could possibly do: he attempted to turn an obvious issue of simple decency into one of the great, wrenching issues of our age. He said he and Indians owner Paul Dolan would "revisit the issue" of the appropriateness of Chief Wahoo in the off-season, as if an image born from one of the most racist periods in American history required further review, discussion, caucusing or, worse, some form of canvassing of an indigenous tribe to determine if it was offended by the use of the logo. It was as if the accomplished, Ivy League–educated commissioner of a $10 billion industry had no common sense of his own.

Why Native Americans receive this treatment speaks directly to the American heart, its refusal to see itself, to own the unique details of its story. The African American, stolen and ruined, has suffered in the United States, and yet today it is generally unacceptable to caricature black people as they once had been. Nor do we refer to women as "secretaries" or "stewardesses," "chicks" or "Toots." Nor, in the movies, do we still smack women in the face to rid them of their female "hysteria." Each is part of an evolution of behavior and language over the past half century to undo what America has been. It is a journey arduous and plodding, insulted and stalled by terms such as "politically correct," but nevertheless it continues. There is no going back to *His Girl Friday*.

The Native American, however, has never been afforded a similar rehabilitation. The lawn jockeys have disappeared but the Chief Wahoos have not. The Sambos are gone but the Braves remain. Save for music, there are no more *niggers* in the everyday public discourse, the adults reduced to scolded children for using the N-word, but Americans, black and white, Latino and Asian, will fight to protect—or do nothing to prevent—the word "Redskins," of no use in America. I suspect the reason for this lack of protection is the Native American has never been the white man's burden but his conquered foe, the spoil to be tortured and erased in life and ridiculed on film and on football helmets and hockey sweaters in death. Americans largely refuse to apologize for slavery, still engaging in clever gymnastics to explain the permanent black underclass. Similarly, to change the names Braves, Indians, and Seminoles, to restore native peoples' dignity, would be to apologize for America itself, for the genocide of a people that created it, for the death march across a continent that created its empire. Americans don't think there is anything to apologize for.

Black Americans were the enslaved, kidnapped people, not the conquered enemy, and thus ownership of them required at some point a restoration, a rehabilitation. The conquered foe remained owned, quarantined, and unrecognized. The Atlanta Braves Baseball Club was founded in 1876, first located in Boston. Ten years earlier, the Civil Rights Act of 1866 and the ratification of the Fourteenth Amendment guaranteed the citizenship of anyone born on the soil of the United States—except Native Americans. The act states that "All persons born in the United States and not subject to any foreign power, excluding Indians not taxed, are hereby declared to be citizens of the United

States," as Martha S. Jones writes in *Birthright Citizens*.[2] The Cleveland Indians were founded as part of the American League in 1901. The following year, the federal government continued its erasure of the native people. "In 1902, Congress accelerated the transfer of land from Indians to whites: a new law required that all allotted lands, upon the death of the owners, be sold at public auction by the heirs, historian Ronald Takaki noted in his classic, *A Different Mirror*. "Unless they were able to purchase their own family lands, Indians would lose what had been their property. . . . Thus, Indian allotments were no longer protected from white land purchasers."[3] Native Americans, people now replaced by monuments, were not even officially recognized as American citizens, and only then grudgingly, until 1924—four years after the Indians had won their first World Series. To the predominately white public (and the black fans going to Redskins games wearing face paint and headdresses, clearly selective in what humiliations they will allow), the Native American team names are more precious, more American than the people who occupied the soil long before them. In the eyes of the government—which, ten years before the baseball team was founded, reduced Indian land in America by 17.4 million acres—the Cleveland Indians have been American longer than the Shawnee, Comanche, Wampanoag, Pueblo, and Hopi. Here first, they are now renters.

Two years later, Manfred offered a milky compromise, forcing the Indians to remove the logo from their uniforms while allowing merchandise to contain the image. The *New York Times* covered the opening of the season the way the white mainstream invariably approaches issues of obvious racial injustice, as the neutral arbiter, treating racism as a simple preference or not as racism at all, without blood or humiliation. It's merely just a difference of opinion, one side preferring a Big Mac, the other a Whopper. "As Cleveland Indians Prepare to Part with Chief Wahoo, Tensions Reignite," a *Times* April 9, 2018, headline read. The story detailed exchanges with fans, as if each owned an equally legitimate claim, Indians fans yelling at protestors to "get a grip." The *Times* solidified its ostensible neutrality by referring to the grinning, dishonest image of Chief Wahoo as it would the Confederate flag, merely as a symbol "that some consider racist."

Manfred took the question of Chief Wahoo that day with a head shake and a flash of temper, as if he were the one being inconvenienced by baseball's willful racism. He didn't want to deal with the insult that Native Americans have been forced to swallow daily, whether the insult is the exploitation of their image whenever the Chicago Blackhawks take to the ice, the insult of their culture turned into a party for white people, the insult of having indignity framed as debate, or knowing that the American mainstream has so chosen an ownership of them that it is willing to fight to preserve its right to perpetually humiliate them. And when the 2018 baseball playoffs began and Cleveland lost to Houston, on the left shoulder of the team uniforms was a patch of Chief Wahoo, a red-faced, grinning, conniving *fuck you* to natives everywhere.

There is a difference between *difficult* and *complicated*, and the issue of removing Native Americans as caricatures from sports teams might be *difficult* because the white men in charge have no interest doing so or lack the courage required to retire top-selling images or to confront the appearance of succumbing to public pressure, of being told what to do, and to alienate the overwhelmingly white season-ticket base, which cares more what a mascot means to them more than what it actually means. It might be difficult for owners to overcome their own racism and the racism embedded into their nostalgia. All of these things may be difficult but they are not complicated. If their degrees have any meaning at all, Rob Manfred and his peers, the other rich-white-man commissioners, know this, too: the mascots must go.

RENTERS

I returned to Boston in 2002. Between college and the start of my professional career I had been gone for seventeen years, and I came back to the city along the pathway predicted years earlier by my high school guidance counselor, who told me of Boston's hierarchy directly, and what it meant for my prospects. "If you're black, you'll never get an opportunity in Boston," he said. "You can't work your way up. You have to go away and build your career, come back with a reputation, and *then* the city will claim you."

Looking for an apartment, I told my wife to prepare for a particular dynamic: "Just be ready," I said. "There's going to be some white people who won't rent to us under any circumstances, some who won't because I'm with you, and some who will *only* because I'm with you. They would never rent to me on my own but to them, your being white will legitimize me." She was Dutch, had never lived in the United States, and, contrary to the belief of so many Americans, had no particular fascination with or desire to be in America or to become a citizen.

Two days and two and a half dozen apartments later, we were disappointed about not getting the place we loved on Tremont Street but ultimately pleased with the place we did get, a brownstone between Columbus and Tremont, at 476 Massachusetts Avenue. In between, she was stunned by the experience, such as the moment we were on Washington Street and drove into Roxbury, Boston's historically black community where my parents were raised. My mother and her two brothers lived with my grandmother at 998 Tremont, not far from Slade's, the restaurant Celtics legend Bill Russell once owned. In the car I made a comment about crossing into Roxbury. It was bait to see how our white real estate agent would respond. Not knowing I was a Bostonian, he immediately reassured me that we were still in the South End and that he would never show us property in Roxbury, where the dangerous black people lived. "I would never *do* that to you guys," he said.

My wife was struck by the way the well-meaning white-woman property managers addressed only her, as if I were the foreigner. At first it appeared to be the old real estate custom of impressing the woman because no deal can be closed with an unhappy wife, but she then noticed that while they chatted her up, enamored by the lilt of her accent and broken English, I was literally ignored during the entirety of several appointments. She did not understand: I was the American. I had the job. I had the money and the career. They were well aware of this. I was the only person on the lease. Only my credit was being checked. Yet in person I was invisible. Despite the geographical fails, they spoke to her as if she were from the Old Country ("What language is that? Dutch? Oh, wow. I've never been to Denmark."), a lineage and familiarity back to the Europe that connects white America. We were in my country. I told her that to them, just by being white, she was more American than I. She was European, I was a renter.

I was not invisible. It was more insidious than that. I was the conduit, her vehicle to becoming American. Within the small talk the requisite connections were being made, effortless links from America to Europe. While I counted the number of electrical outlets in the living room and inspected the water pressure of the shower, the owners were talking. *I'm one-thirty-sixth Dutch. My great-grandfather was from Haarlem . . . Do you live close to Amsterdam? Maybe we're, like, related. Wouldn't that be wild?* I was home, again, in the city of my birth, but no familiar links were being made to me, even though one of the agents and I grew up just a few towns over from each other. These streets and the memories they produced—from Where's Boston to Lena Park, Egleston Station to Simco's—were mine. And yet, here, I was merely the resource for my wife's future Americanness, and whether or not it was a club she wanted to join, if the time ever came when she needed the club—and that time *did* come—whiteness would be there for her. And it was. She was on her way to becoming an owner and I didn't just watch them roll out the welcome mat for her, I paid for it.

She was outraged at the unfairness of it all, a mild, temporary, and *welcome* protection of me, but quite possibly her outrage stemmed from her initial disbelief of what I said she would encounter. To her, like so many white people, such racism was obviously preposterous, and until she saw it firsthand she figured I was simply being dramatic, paranoid. *People just don't act that way.* From disbelief to anger to opportunism, she had experienced the full scope of the hoax of whiteness, the hoax of America.

THE HOAX OF WHITENESS

When it became clearer that a Trump presidency was a real possibility (and make no mistake: his election *was* a mandate of whiteness), a shocking number of my frightened, well-meaning, progressive friends concluded that "identity politics" was what drove otherwise well-meaning white people into his arms. The attitude was a common one nationwide, an episode of logic surrendering to emotion.

Good progressives—women, blacks (especially blacks at only 13 percent of the population), queers, Latinos—recognize that political and social progress requires alliances and they know that identity politics is a derogatory term used to deflect attention from the desire to maintain white identity as the American default.

But they also understand the delicate nature of the challenge: to cultivate support from other progressives without crossing that invisible line that makes allies flee. The historical limits of these alliances are very well known and the alliances thrive only under one condition: when whiteness is allowed to remain unquestioned, and more importantly, unthreatened.

Identity politics shatters the boundaries and when the mainstream grows annoyed by its existence it should, for it is a threat. It is not a request. It is a sword. It does not assume the inherent superiority or wisdom of whiteness but in its defiance demands equality of thought and status. It demands that the people in charge—white people, straight people, and, for women, the men—relinquish power. The concept of alliance suddenly shifts from support out of charitable impulse without their status being threatened to having power taken from them. It is not being asked to share, but being ordered to. Identity politics is a form of reparation but it is much more than that. It is a declaration of revolution. It is a reimagining of who is in charge.

Knowing the boundaries of the whites tired of the blacks still pushing for things, of the women sick of the feminists asking for too much, of the blacks who know reimagining is unrealistic, of the straights who cannot figure out why one's homosexuality must be a public issue instead of a private one, minority progressives know when the line is being crossed, when the white moderates with the good intentions are beginning their inevitable retreat. Minority progressives are reminded that the maintaining of whiteness is a condition of the white moderate's alliance after all and must remain the default. Then, we can be friends. These allies want to be supportive but only to a point. They don't want to be reimagined, and the push itself has now become the enemy. Thus, the progressives retrench and preemptively curb their ambitions and tone before their white allies flee. It is a strategic retreat.

They also know, perhaps even more fearfully, that such a relationship could hardly be called an alliance if asserting one's live, physical presence is all it takes to turn a supporter into a Trump voter. Within these limits, if they indeed can be called limits, black and female progressives are stuck, unable to survive without support from sympathetic moderates but also unable to express themselves. The result is being constantly on the defensive. White itself is not a color nor an identity, while women voting with a #MeToo sensibility are accused of identity politics. The only thing more insane than this position is the number of black people and women who so readily repeat it.

The liberal, elevated, and, above all, Ivy-smart *New Yorker* magazine fell flush into this trap on September 24, 2018, when reporter Hua Hsu reviewed the Clay Travis book *Republicans Buy Sneakers, Too: How the Left Is Ruining Sports with Politics.* It was Curt Schilling–Steve Deace all over again. Travis was profiled with the typical *New Yorker* touches—flattery of at least questionable traits. (Hsu describes Travis's truther streak and obvious reinforcements of whiteness and its standard as "speaking his mind with a confrontational verve.") The headline of the article, "Should Politics Be Kept Out of Sports?," asked a seemingly innocuous, neutral question but using Travis and his right-wing reaction as the story's test-case hypothesis implied he was somehow apolitical, pure, objective when both the book's subtitle and its cover (an illustration of Donald Trump dunking a basketball over Colin Kaepernick) frame his argument in the most obvious and unsubtle political way: in the usual left-right, Hatfield-McCoy terms. He is allowed, however, to have his book—an obviously political counterpoint to the politics he resents, with all the predictable targets attacked—be treated as impartial.

The assumption of neutrality is the hoax of whiteness. It is positioned as probing, asking questions without motive. Hsu does not once in his review suggest that Travis's book is entirely political. Travis even argues, unchallenged by the writer, another discredited conservative claim: that the laws of the United States discriminate in favor of black people based on their skin color. Hsu, a Harvard grad and Taiwanese American writer, and the *New Yorker*, the high-brow, erudite magazine of legend, let him get away with saying this. Hsu allowed Travis the authoritative platform of an owner while reducing his traditional targets back to renters. Travis uses all the conservative tropes throughout the book and the piece—*identity politics, left-wing liberal, affirmative action*—unsubtle and shallow, tired and hypocritical, and yet he is allowed to be considered reasonable. As Naomi Klein would say, it is quite a con.

All of which returns one to the same conclusion: there is no power in being American. There is only power in being white.

On our best days we like to believe the opposite is true, that there is no such thing as color, there is only being American. If this were true, white Americans would not believe they can wantonly revoke citizenship from nonwhite Americans.

Periodically, there have been moments of retrofitting, precious snatches of victory, a sense that maybe there was a rent-to-own provision somewhere in the lease. In their veins, proven by the many backlashes to others' victories, white people consider themselves the only true Americans and they will decide to whom they will rent and for how long. They will decide to Tomahawk Chop—or not. A black Olympian does a victory lap, the American flag draped around her shoulders, and never quite becomes a true American, but a black athlete who chooses not to play for her country or questions it is guaranteed to become an *un*-American. The thousands of black men who fought in all the wars—Revolutionary, Civil, the two Great Wars, and all the conflicts outside of and in between—don't become more American; they are still identified first as black. A black citizen who challenges police under the premise of being an American or under the premise of being an owner finds out very quickly that he is only but a renter. The words on the parchment do not apply to him and do not give him the right to an opinion. They never did. He has been here but only on the lease. Never on the deed.

The hoax of America lies in the fiction that it wants to be America without first being white. The nation trumpets its limitlessness even as so many of its white citizens believe ever more strongly in their right to decide who gets to stay and who must leave. Give one's life in battle. Win the gold medal. Make the all-defining money. Build the charter school. While America repeats the aspirational rhetoric that there is always something the nonwhite renter can do to become an owner, the future of black people lies not in the demand that the rhetoric be fulfilled but in the recognition that surviving this hostile territory finally means no longer having to listen to it at all.

ACKNOWLEDGMENTS

There is, quite plainly, a war against black people in this country. We will be tolerated if we do not speak, do not challenge, and appear grateful for everything we have, grateful that our lives are not worse. Our successes are treated as opportunities given and not earned. We do not have the right to address injustices or imbalances, regardless of their historical and statistical obviousness, and when we do the campaigns to smother, discredit, and ignore our perspectives are immediate and unrelenting. Against this backdrop of hostility in reality, I am grateful for the opportunity to speak. As so many writers know, being published is not a given.

Many thanks to Helene Atwan, Pamela McColl, Alyssa Hassan, and the entire team at Beacon Press for always being enthusiastic about promoting and supporting the work. Having worked together on two books now, I know that any author working with Rakia Clark as their editor is a lucky one. So many of the concepts in this originated in the pages of *ESPN the Magazine*. Scott Burton, Rebecca Hudson, and Jena Janovy have always been encouraging journalistic voices to challenging our assumptions and conventions, especially on subjects that are not particularly popular to the corners of the sports world who only want the final score.

I am always thankful for a wonderful inner circle who helped shape and refine thoughts and were gracious enough with their time to look at sections of the manuscript. David Kutzmann has been a peerless editor for two decades of book projects. Many phone calls, lunches, and dinners with Tisa Bryant, Christopher Sauceda, Peg Kern, Glenn Stout, Laura Harrington, and my agent, Deirdre Mullane at Mullane Literary, turned ideas into paragraphs. Molly Yanity has my thanks for reading portions of the manuscript and I am grateful for John Hoberman, who is like a walking clipping service. Important conversations with Toni Smith-Thompson, whose ideas and perspectives on race, class, and the chilling, increased presence of police in our schools and communities, are deeply interwoven within these pages.

I am grateful to the writers who inspire me to write, whose phrases do not belong to me but have often found their way into my work because they are so good, so appropriate. The term "magical thinking" stayed with me after reading Joan Didion's *The Year of Magical Thinking*. In considering the runaway grift and graft of the millionaires Donald Trump installed in his cabinet to profit from and weaken the government, I use the term "spectacular con," which Naomi Klein used perfectly in *No Is Not Enough*. On two occasions, the phrase "There are many ways to tell a lie" appears in the text, which is a shout-out to Rebecca Solnit, who captured the sly practice with those words in her essay "Politics and the American Language," the foreword to her essay collection *Call Them by Their True Names*.

Part of the writing journey is finding comfort with the organic places it will take you. There is a war against black people in this country but there is also a massive assault against truth and poor people and ethics. These times feel dark and defining. Friendships and relationships have been tested. Some have survived. Others have not. If the times have felt like a severing, a bitter reckoning with Trump and a country that increasingly embraces white nationalism, reckless capitalism, and sustained racial incuriosity, they also represent an opportunity to explore what lies in front of us with different eyes, with new people who share similar values. I am grateful for the inner circle that remains intact and for the new voices that have joined it. We will start a new story together. Or, as they say in Spanish, *juntos*.

NOTES

WHAT COLIN KAEPERNICK TAUGHT US

1. Felicia Sonmez, "Trump Suggests That Protesting Should Be Illegal, *Washington Post*, September 5, 2018, https://www.washingtonpost.com/politics/trump-suggests-protesting-should-be-illegal/2018/09/04/11cfd9be-b0a0-11e8-aed9-001309990777_story.html?noredirect=on&utm_term=.17af1870bd41.

IT'S OK TO CRITICIZE THE MILITARY

1. Defense Logistics Agency, "1033 Program FAQs," https://www.dla.mil/DispositionServices/Offers/Reutilization/Law Enforcement/ProgramFAQs.aspx.

2. John McCain and Jeff Flake, *Tackling Paid Patriotism: A Joint Oversight Report by U.S. Sens. John McCain and Jeff Flake* (Washington, DC: US Senate, 2017).

3. Melvin A. Goodman, *National Insecurity: The Cost of American Militarism* (San Francisco: City Lights Books, 2013), 144.

4. Neta C. Crawford, *The Costs of War: United States Budgetary Costs of Post-9/11 Wars Through FY2018* (Providence: Watson Institute of International & Public Affairs, Brown University, November 2017), 3.

5. Goodman, *National Insecurity*, 316–17.

6. Crawford, *The Costs of War*, 7.

7. Goodman, *National Insecurity*, 33.

THE LOST TRIBE OF INTEGRATION

1. Barry Bluestone and Mary Huff Stevenson, *The Boston Renaissance: Race, Space, and Economic Change in an American Metropolis* (New York: Russell Sage Foundation, 2000), 190.

THE MEDIOCRE WHITE BOY

1. Leanne E. Atwater et al., "Looking Ahead: How What We Know about Sexual Harassment Now Informs Us of the Future," *Organizational Dynamics* (2018), https://doi.org/10.1016/j.orgdyn.2018.08.008.

2. Laila Robbins and Alicia Bannon et al., *State Supreme Court Diversity: Across the Country, Courts Fail to Reflect the Racial, Ethnic, and Gender Diversity of the Communities They Serve* (New York: Brennan Center for Justice, New York University School of Law, July 23, 2019), https://www.brennancenter.org/publication/state-supreme-court-diversity.

3. *The Asian American Vote 2016: A Report by the Asian American Legal Defense and Education Fund* (New York: AALDEF, 2017), https://www.aaldef.org/uploads/TheAsianAmericanVote2016-AALDEF.pdf; "Exit Polls," Election 2016, CNN Politics, updated November 23, 2016, https://www.cnn.com/election/2016/results/exit-polls/national/president.

RENTERS

1. Carol Anderson, *White Rage: The Unspoken Truth of Our Racial Divide* (New York: Bloomsbury, 2016), 3.

2. Martha S. Jones, *Birthright Citizens: A History of Race and Rights in Antebellum America* (Cambridge, UK: Cambridge University Press, 2018), 47.

3. Ronald Takaki, *A Different Mirror: A History of Multicultural America* (New York: Back Bay, 2008), 237.